FINDERS
KEEPERS

FINDERS KEEPERS

A Practical Approach To Find And Keep
Your Writing Critique Partner

JOY E. RANCATORE & MEAGAN SMITH

LOGOS & MYTHOS PRESS

SLIDELL, LA, USA

FINDERS KEEPERS: A PRACTICAL APPROACH TO FIND AND KEEP YOUR WRITING CRITIQUE PARTNER
Copyright © 2019 by **Joy E. Rancatore** and **Meagan Smith**
Cover Design, Layout and Interior Graphics by **Rachael Ritchey**, RR Publishing
Edited by **Joy E. Rancatore**
www.logosandmythospress.com

All rights reserved. No part of this book may be reproduced or transmitted in any form or by any electronic or mechanical means, including photocopying, recording or information storage and retrieval systems, without written permission of the publisher, except for the use of brief quotations in a book review or where permitted by law. For permissions contact: editorial@logosandmythospress.com.

Note: We use the masculine pronoun for simplicity.
Permission: *Mention of two of their fabulous flavors allowed by kind permission of Blue Bell Creameries.*
Disclaimers: *We are not lawyers or CPAs and make no claims to give legal, contractual or financial advice in this book. We also cannot answer any questions on those topics. Likewise, we are not counselors or psychologists and cannot give clinical advice. Because ours is an emotional profession, mental and emotional discoveries often occur as we dive into our work or seek to understand our motivations, fears and needs. Any information we share along these lines comes from our own experiences. If you uncover deep emotional turmoil or trauma at any point during the reading of this book or while working through the challenges, we urge you to seek professional guidance. Counselors are fantastic sources of help for those times. We are cheering you on and want you to know we have faced many emotions—high and low—through our individual creative journeys.*

ISBN 13: 978-1-7331387-3-4 (paperback)
ISBN 13: 978-1-7331387-4-1 (e-book)
Library of Congress Control Number:2019956142

Logos & Mythos Press LLC
Slidell, LA, USA

To the Critique Partners who have yet to find one another;

And to those who've met their keepers.

Table of Contents

Acknowledgments   *i*
Note to Reader   *vii*
Introduction   *xi*

CHAT ONE: **Defining Critique Partnerships**   3

Our first chat focuses on what a critique partnership is and isn't, as well as the purposes and benefits of a well-founded critique relationship.

CHAT TWO: **Evaluating Yourself for Your New Role**   33

We chat about how a writer can know when he's ready to become a critique partner, evaluating himself through three lenses: intellectual, emotional and practical.

CHAT THREE: **Choosing a Critique Partner**   63

Our partnership stems from part luck, part hard work and full commitment. In this chat, we share ways you can seek out your own partner and build your relationship on a solid foundation or strengthen the partnership you already have.

CHAT FOUR: **Preparing for a Critique**   105

Communication centers a partnership. We provide you with some specific definitions in this chat, along with some questions to ask and answer with your partner before you exchange critique expectations.

CHAT FIVE: **Giving a Critique**   151

We had no idea how to give a critique when we got started, so this chat breaks down lessons we've learned through our experiences, in hopes you don't have to spend time finding these nuggets on your own.

CHAT SIX: **Receiving a Critique**   197

Any critique—no matter how kind and well-intentioned—will sting. We share our tips for accepting, processing and utilizing a critique to make us better writers with stronger words.

Conclusion   215

QWERTY Friends   223
   Candice Marley Conner & Carrie Dalby   224
   Karen Hugg & Natasha Oliver   234
   Autumn Lindsey & Amanda Linsmeier   244
   Jamie Raintree & Aimie Runyan   252
   Kelsey Atkins, Tauri Cox, Devon Harry & Joy E. Rancatore   262

Appendix A: Collection of QWERTY Tips   273
Appendix B: Strengths & Weaknesses Challenge   279
Appendix C: Critique Partner Interview Questionnaire   282
Appendix D: Critique Structure Questionnaire   287
Appendix E: Surviving Writing Critique Groups   290
Appendix F: Mea's Theory of Fear   306
Appendix G: Joy's Time Tips   311
Appendix H: Joy's Case For Goals   321
Appendix I: QWERTY-Recommended Resources   328
Appendix J: Critique Partner Contract   336
Glossary of QWERTY Definitions   339
Sources   346
About the Author: Joy E. Rancatore   348
About the Author: Meagan Smith   350

QWERTY Speaking Availability   352
QWERTY Writing Life Podcast   353
Logos & Mythos Press Editing Services   354

Acknowledgments
From the QWERTYs

THANK YOU TO OUR book team. We are humbled and ecstatic to walk alongside you all on this author dream.
- Cover and graphics designer Rachael Ritchey, whose unfailing kindness, immense patience and boundless creativity made our words a work of art.
- Our advisor and mentor, Allison Chestnut, who helped us form our thoughts into a conversation that came from our hearts.
- Our special editor, Thad, whose insights and great ideas slayed us.
- Our beta readers—Carrie Dalby, Candice Marley Conner and Kelsey Atkins—who encouraged us, made us better and solidified that our message was worthy.
- The critique partners who trusted us enough to put their names and thoughts in our spotlight section—Devon Harry, Tauri Cox, Kelsey Atkins, Aimie Runyan, Jamie Raintree, Amanda Linsmeier, Autumn Lindsey, Natasha Oliver, Karen Hugg, Carrie Dalby and Candice Marley

Conner. We're proud of each one of you and blessed to call you our QWERTY Friends.
- Early reviewers and launch team heroes, whose kind words and online presence help the larger writing community find our book.

To the fans of QWERTY Writing Life podcast who have blessed us with your kindness, curiosity and conversation—thank you. We hope you love this book as much as you love our show, if not more!

Thank you to all the authors seeking to better your craft and searching to find your CP for keeps. We're so honored you chose us to help you on your mission.

To our Ninjas—we may be a secret group, but we aim for people to know your name. Thank you for giving us a shot of encouragement and for standing behind our book's purpose with enough faith to say, "I'd like to try that again."

From Meagan

WRITING THIS BOOK HAS pushed me farther as an author than I've ever gone before. It's crazy hard to put what's in my mind on paper in a way other people can understand. This project tapped into and exercised a part of my brain that was underused. It's feeling rather healthy now, though!

Thank you to Joy who modeled what dreaming out loud looks like and then asked me to sing along.

Thank you to Allison who reminded us to stay true to our identity, which happened to also be our strength. This book didn't *feel* like mine until that moment, and I'm so proud of the outcome.

Thank you to Brent for all the patience and support. I'm going to get personal for a moment because he deserves that, folks. B, your faith in my ability to finish and finish well floors me every time I think about it. You had to live in the day-to-day chaos, and you actively listened to me talk in a jargon that was foreign to you. You picked up household jobs that slipped through my fingers while I focused on writing things. During revisions weeks, you sacrificed quality time with me, so I could hang out with the manuscript. You watched our children while I sat at book festivals, guest-lectured in classrooms, took days off to write and met with other authors. All the while you fulfilled your responsibilities with your business and your friends. You're more than a partner. You're my best friend, and you're my Favorite.

Thank you to Clay and Cole, my two boys, for waking me up. Thank you for inspiring me and making me laugh and showing me how deeply I can love. Because of you both, I'm taking responsibility for my professional life, so I can be a proper role model … so I can be the one who shows you how to reach for dreams rather than just telling you that you should. I'm selfish enough to say that I want you to learn that from me. From other people, too—that's fine—but mostly from me.

Thank you to the OG Dreamers: Amy Tolley who introduced me to *Twilight* and Maggie Stiefvater who is an endless inspiration to me. To Maggie Farrell who has always been a creative muse through college and beyond. To mom who raised me and watched my boys while Joy and I pounded out a first draft that weekend in June. To Brandon and MK for always wanting to dream a little dream with me. You all bring me joy, and my life is so much better with you in it.

Since I told them I wanted to be an author, Daniel Caldwell and Brett Golson have been beyond supportive. I am so happy to work with these gentlemen on the daily. Thank you.

Thank you to my Savior, Jesus Christ, for his love, sacrifice and redemption. If I had nothing, I'd still have everything because of Him.

From Joy

GREATEST THANKS TO GOD for the gift of words and the opportunities to use them for him.

Thank you to Tony who repeatedly told me, "I believe in what you're doing." You made all the hard work behind the scenes possible through your support and encouragement and by picking up my slack around our house.

Thank you to my kids who put up with this crazy author life.

Thank you to Mea for being brave enough to say "Yes!" to my crazy plans, for being patient enough to work with me and for being wise enough to know when to guide me to a better way. Thank you for learning this CP thing with me!

Thank you to my critique partners for being my CP unicorns. Devon, Kelsey and Tauri, you exemplify everything CPs should be. I am thankful to have you in my life—not just as fellow writers who make me better—but also as three of the greatest friends a girl could dream of having. I was blessed to find you ladies, and I'm in it for keeps!

Thank you to my family at Northside Baptist Church for supporting and encouraging me always. "I thank my God upon every remembrance of you ...." Philippians 1:3

Note to Reader

Dearest Reader,

THANK YOU FOR PICKING UP our book. We hope it inspires, emboldens, enlightens and drives you. You'll find this book is arranged differently from most writing craft books. We follow the style of our weekly podcast, QWERTY Writing Life, where we chat candidly with each other to relay information to you—whether it's a personal struggle, a lesson learned or a reflection on the creative lives we lead.

We invite you to join our conversation by participating in the QWERTY Challenges located at the end of each section—like our parting gift to listeners of each podcast episode.

This is the book we needed a few years ago. We had reconnected after a decade apart, both in the same mindset of pursuing our passions as lifelong career goals. We wanted to help each other as critique partners but had no idea how to do that.

When our research turned up little clarity, we dove in to this new partnership with four vital characteristics: honesty, openness, a willingness to learn and a desire to aid one another in our pursuits. After trial and error and a few stumbles along our critiquing journey, we felt the ground solidify beneath us and had a few laughs over how we should write the book we couldn't find.

Finders Keepers is the result of that joking declaration, combined with a realization that, surely, we weren't the only writers needing it. This book contains an interview between two writers who accidentally did something right. In each chat, we—the QWERTYs—examine a different aspect of the critique partnership.

Because we're practical girls, we include tangible steps to process what you learn and discover. What's the point of tens of thousands of words strung together and bound up in a pretty package if they don't produce introspection or action?

You'll need a place to store your answers to the challenges. We suggest you combine this book with a notebook. Look at it this way: we're actually encourageing you to buy a shiny new notebook. Grab a few pens while you're at it. Maybe some sticky tabs, highlighters, cute paperclips .... What can we say? The office supply store is our happy place.

Note to Readers   ix

After your shopping trip, you'll discover opportunities to journal as you work through this book. You might uncover unexpected truths about yourself; some might require outside guidance to flesh out, if they open deep wounds. If you're new to this topic or to writing in general, you may find parts of this book overwhelming. Understand that the tips and suggestions we make are ones that have worked for us or others. They may or may not fit your situation or style. You should take our critiquing advice piece by piece, try what makes sense and discard what doesn't work for you.

We recommend you gather or create three to five short stories or articles similar to the types of writing you'd like to have critiqued. You'll use them during some of our challenges. These pieces and your notebook should be all you need to gain the most from this book.

Each reader of this book will complete it at his own pace. Whether yours is slow or fast, we hope you find your perfect critique partner at the right time or grow together with your current partner in the best way for your relationship. If this whole critiquing business feels overwhelming and unattainable, flip the page.

Happy Reading!

Joy & Mea

Joy & Mea

Introduction

MEA: Hi, I'm Meagan, but everyone calls me Mea.

JOY: And, I'm Joy. Together we founded QWERTY Writing Life podcast and this Author Resource Series of books. We've been writers forever, friends since college and critique partners since we made active leaps of faith to pursue creative publication.

What Makes This Book Special?

MEA: *Finders Keepers* offers writers a candid explanation of the critique partner relationship. The book includes a working definition for the partnership and addresses who this relationship is for, how it can operate and why it's important. The book gives you a common starting point, whether you're new to the concept or eager to strengthen an existing team.

JOY: We're not stopping there, though. We include practical applications through our QWERTY Challenges to transform this information into action when paired with the right person (or people) in your critique corner and the correct mindset from you. You could be part of an unstoppable team whose members launch words into the world in a more powerful, polished manner. You're not alone anymore.

MEA: Finding the right critique partner could quicken the development of writing craft skills, teach you how to help others without hurting them and develop a friendship with a fellow writer who understands your struggles and situation. We think that's a special opportunity.

Why Did We Write This Book?

JOY: We needed this book. We committed to one another at the start of this adventure to be each other's champions and critique partners, to hold one another accountable and to nudge each other toward achieving our dreams. My evaluation of Mea's poetry chap book was step one. Suddenly, we were critique partners.

MEA: Next, Joy drafted a short story, then a novel. The short story couldn't intimidate me. The novel, on the other hand, ... totally different tale.

In theory, the whole critique process seemed self-explanatory. Read the piece; point out the rough patches; go out for tacos. I felt confident in my knowledge, but I'd been burned by that feeling before—specifically, when writing my first novel. I remember sitting down, opening a document and typing *Chapter One,* believing my ability to read and write and consume story made me capable of intuitively producing a good book. And, all the authors laughed. No, this critiquing business felt deceptively easy. I knew from my experience of drafting a novel that, as with that endeavor, many hidden steps would also lead me to the inner room of critiquing.

Another cause for hesitation was the realization I would not just inhibit myself if I failed. My mind produced a domino effect scenario—Mea gives Joy bad advice; Joy implements bad advice; Joy gets assaulted by objectors of bad advice; Joy ends up strapped to a pillar to be tarred and feathered; so on and so forth.

JOY: I may not admit the drama that played out in my mind—pitchforks and flames featured prominently—but I, also, decided such an undertaking required examination. Considering it took me a week to research the right travel carrier for my precious Tolkien Cat, I knew this would be no short research trip and deserved my due diligence.

MEA: Our research dug up a few tips. For example, one website suggested the author should clarify what he expected his critique partner to do. I was confused. I thought the title *critique partner* articulated my needs. Ummm ... critique my book? Is there another way to say that?

JOY: Another suggestion equally perplexed me: know the theme and mood of the book. My theme was still up in the air. I hoped Mea could help me work through that. The mood, you say? Well, my book's feeling ... grumpy, bashful, sleepy?

MEA: Remember this tip, Joy? "Have fun!" We might ... if we knew what the heck we were doing!

What little information we found contained good suggestions but no practical application—much like holding a map filled with destinations but finding no roads to follow. We set aside our research and pieced together a plan to get Joy's novel a decent critique.

JOY: We had successes and failures but felt confident we improved the book. With a revised plan, we tried again on Mea's novel and thought, *We're getting better at this!*

Continued refinement of our critique process came through short fiction, nonfiction and poetry, as we communicated each hit and miss along the way. We discovered a rhythm for critiquing that consistently works for us, and this partnership has taken our writing to a higher level quicker than if we were alone.

MEA: While reminiscing about the beginning of our critique journey and munching on chocolate chip cookies, we laughed about the missteps we took while turning this amorphous thing into something tangible and shiny. One of us—I can't remember who—said, "I wish I'd known at the beginning what I know now. It would have saved us so much darn trouble."

Our eyes widened; our brains sparked. We became more observant of the writing community. Turns out, a lot of writers wanted the same thing. We'd seen the boundless benefits in our own experience and wanted the same for our fellow writers, so this book was born.

Who Is This Book For?

JOY: Every moderately practiced writer seeking to improve his abilities through a critique partnership should gain value from this book. If you are an experienced critique partner (CP), you can use this book for validation that your relationship is at its best or for the purpose of improving it.

MEA: Also, if you've never had a critique partner, but you've recently heard about them or you desire to search for one, you can use this book as a guide. Cultivating a healthy relationship from the beginning will probably save you frustration. This book contains a proven plan you can alter to your needs, instead of starting from scratch like we did.

JOY: We hope you'll still consider this topic if you're skeptical of the process or have had unpleasant critique experiences. We believe that once you find your person or people, you'll hold a priceless partnership.

MEA: Going through this book with your person and sharing answers to the QWERTY Challenges can spark heart-to-heart chats. If you don't have that person now, you can flip back through this book with him once you've met.

Why Now?

JOY: Questions pertaining to critique partners frequent writers' groups and forums:
- What are critique partners?

- Are they the same as beta readers, advanced readers, book coaches, editors or reviewers? If not, what's the difference?
- Do I even need one?
- Where can I find one?
- If I find one, what do I do with him?
- This is the one that breaks our hearts—I've had critique partners in the past, and they broke my spirit. How do I move past that?

MEA: When we looked for answers to these same questions, we couldn't find one resource that explored this crucial writing relationship in depth and mapped out how to do it well. Confusion abounds regarding what critique partners should and shouldn't be.

We aim to clarify.

JOY: With the rise of independent publication, the book market overflows. It may be more important than ever to make what's between the covers remarkable in order to stand out. Both independently and traditionally published authors want the best product for editors and readers. Because we're stronger with people we trust on our team, critique partners can make us outstanding.

MEA: Since this process works on a barter system—I make your book better; you make mine better—such a relationship is also cost-effective. A critique partner potentially reduces an editor's time, ensuring a deeper edit and quicker release and establishing your reputation as a knowledgeable author. As a confidante with whom you discuss writing craft, emotions and wonder, your critique partner can increase the rate at which you learn craft techniques. In the end, you might produce better work, more quickly; thereby meeting the needs of our fast-paced publishing world.

JOY: The primary *why now* for *Finders Keepers* is the informational gap regarding critique partnerships. We wanted to fill that void, because most everything we know came by piecing together scattered internet information with our own trial and error. Our hope is for this book to be a go-to, comprehensive resource that will strengthen current partner relationships and build strong new ones.

A critique partnership ripe with respect, knowledge, effort and communication can help both you and your partner get where you want to be faster with greater proficiency.

Now is the perfect time to start ... together.

QWERTY CHAT

Defining Critique Partnerships

CHAT ONE: Defining Critique Partnerships

OUR FIRST CHAT FOCUSES on what a critique partnership is and isn't, as well as the purposes and benefits of a well-founded critique relationship.

SECTION I: EXPLANATIONS OF A CRITIQUE PARTNERSHIP

Why does a critique relationship exist?

JOY: For us, the answer to this question is found in our definition of the critique partner (CP) relationship. We will include QWERTY definitions to CP-related concepts to keep us on the same page and to give you and your partner a common understanding on which to base your communications. As you progress together, you might develop your own definitions.

The **CRITIQUE PARTNER RELATIONSHIP** exists to improve the writer and the writing to the benefit of each person involved in the creative process and for all future readers.

MEA: Once we determined the purpose of this partnership, we examined who should be part of one.

What should a CP look like?

A **CRITIQUE PARTNER** (CP) should be a knowledgeable writer who desires to assist other writers with their works and willingly accepts reciprocation, creating a harmonious relationship that results in literature superior to what the author alone could provide for readers.

JOY: Since this is our most important definition, we will examine each part.

KNOWLEDGEABLE WRITER:

If you choose a critique partner who is not a writer, he will not have the craft tools and knowledge necessary to assist with the order, structure and development of a story. Those tasks are the core of what a critique partner does. This doesn't mean he must know everything. This partnership, properly developed, will lead to an ongoing education for both parties. You will be a far wiser critique partner in ten years than you are now. To get there, though, you must start with some basic understandings and be willing to improve those and learn as you progress—hopefully, together.

A non-writer won't have the emotional tools necessary to provide the full respect and honesty needed. Writing is stereotypically undervalued. Often, a seemingly simple piece has hours, days, weeks, possibly months of grinding and perfecting rough edges behind it. If a partner doesn't write, he may not understand that, sometimes, finding that perfect perspective can take weeks and closing that plot hole, even longer. A fellow writer relates to your struggle and celebrates each achievement, like high-fiving a 2:00 a.m. epiphany. For us, this comradery is as important as knowing the craft.

Desires:

MEA: I'm getting blunt with this next explanation. The person you're considering as your critique partner should want to help you with your work. On the other side, he shouldn't consider splashing a mess on paper for someone else to fix. This is selfish and lazy. There. I said it. If your toes hurt because I stepped on them, well, maybe you deserve it.

This relationship requires time, devotion and commitment to each other and to the craft—from both sides. The person who is not willing to dedicate these resources epitomizes the type of person who leaves others with negative feelings toward critique relationships. These partnerships are not all give; nor are they all take. They're both.

Willing reciprocation can be a learned behavior, Friend. If a person isn't naturally giving, he may struggle at first but can still become a valuable CP with the right attitude.

To Assist:

JOY: We designated the word assist when formulating this definition. Words we did not choose include *dominate, impose himself, force* or *commandeer* because they stand contrary to a critique partner's purpose. An advantageous partner will ask questions that require deep thinking about the story. He will also honor the author's vision with his suggestions. A person who becomes upset if his advice isn't implemented in its entirety or who vies for his idea over the author's cannot comprise the second half of a healthy CP relationship.

WILLINGLY ACCEPTS RECIPROCATION:

MEA: Let's take this concept a step further and discuss the need to recognize this partnership as such. Remember our phrase, *willingly accepts*? In addition to sharing ideas and suggestions to improve another writer, a CP should accept critique in order to progress his abilities and polish his writing. As a characteristic, this action manifests as an eagerness to learn, specifically from his partner—a person he hopefully respects. No one writes a perfect story on his first try, and everyone needs help and improvement. If you can't accept that, you can't be critiqued and you can't improve, either. Joy and I believe all writers with this attitude should be sent to the rack.

JOY: Mea!

MEA: Just seeing if they're still with us.

JOY: I'll rephrase that. We believe that writers with this attitude could benefit from an adjusted, more humble perspective, which includes stretching ourselves in an effort to become more flexible and well-rounded as writers.

Our writing—without outside guidance—is inherently flawed and, therefore, proof that you are capable of imperfection. If you choose a partner with this outlook, you will always feel inferior while he is lording above you, brushing his white horse and spit-shining his special event armor. This attitude rejects any conversation on craft that includes your ideas and suggestions. Your growth is stunted, and so is your partner's. He won't notice, but you will. No. You need to be brothers in this endeavor—soldiers, fighting the good fight side by side.

Harmonious Relationship:

MEA: When we work alongside people we trust, we are stronger. The harmony and balance that result from well-matched CPs who strive for clear communication characterize one of the most beautiful writing relationships. It's the giving and receiving of critiques, yes, but each partner must also respect the other. Sometimes this comes with time. Sometimes, for the more skeptical, this unity comes with proof of work or a combination of the two.

LITERATURE SUPERIOR TO WHAT THE AUTHOR ALONE COULD PROVIDE:

JOY: You might be an outstanding writer—the next J.R.R. Tolkien, my favorite author. Even Tolkien needed reproof, correction, urging—and the occasional sharp nudge. You're no different. If C.S. Lewis and other members of the Inklings critique group hadn't pushed Tolkien to let go of his incessant perfecting, he may have never published anything during his lifetime; and his son would have had to posthumously complete and release all his works. The entire concept of the Inklings' meetings was to push one another to produce better literature.

Alone, we might be good; together, we could be brilliant. Critique partners tell the truth in love to raise each other up.

FOR READERS:

MEA: Finally, we think it's important to remember why we're doing all this in the first place. When you began writing, you likely did it for yourself. Maybe you had an audience in mind—bedtime stories for your children—or a purpose for the stories you needed to tell—a literary legacy for someone dear to you. Most likely, you felt the bubbling need to release a story. So, you did; and that was all you needed ... at the time.

JOY: As you grew in your writing and in knowledge of yourself as a writer, you likely had a shift in purpose. This happens differently for every writer; but, somewhere along the way, you veered from a fear of readers to a longing for them. You produced a story. It rose from your imagination or memory or research until it spread its literary wings to soar into the hands and hearts of deserving readers. Because it is precious to you and you want it to be equally dear to them, you desire to send it forth as polished as possible. The CP who honors the writer's vision and audience through his critique aids in this goal.

What Are Some Critique Partner Misconceptions?

MEA: I'm eager to answer this question because many common assumptions don't directly pertain to a critique partnership. Joy, will you list some common misconceptions of who CPs are, and we'll go through them together?

JOY: Sure! Here we go. A critique partner should *not* be:
- Your beta reader
- Your professional editor
- Your book coach

- Your grandmother
- Your bully
- Your servant

MEA: Let us ease your worried mind if you've found your thoughts on this list. You're not alone. We compiled these assumptions by being writing-centered online observers, and all these titles appear repeatedly. We intend to explain why each of these roles are not linked with critiques.

BETA READERS

JOY: The purpose of a beta reader is to get an organic reader's response to your book. A beta reader can be a writer, yes; but that's not a requirement. When a writer is a beta reader, he takes off his writer's dapper top hat and puts on his reader's snuggly beanie. A beta reader will read a near-finished draft of your book that has become the gorgeous specimen it is because of the labor of you, your critique partner(s) and your editor(s). He will tell you if the book reads well, if it holds his attention, if anything gets lost in translation. He can also provide a glimpse into your ideal reader and into some of the reactions you can expect once your book is released.

Critique partners see the good bones of your story and help you apply muscle and skin; beta readers examine your mostly completed creation and help you straighten its clothing.

Professional Editors

MEA: Whether you publish your own work or accept a contract from a publisher, you will—or, we believe, should—work with one or multiple editors. This is in addition to the revision work you do before, during and after your CP's critique. While editors go by different titles, you likely will work with some combination of developmental, legal, copy and line editors and proofreaders.

JOY: Some of the specific roles these professionals will fill for you include your story's big picture needs—plot, structure, characters, development, theme, etc.—you and your CP missed; potential legal or infringement details—copyrights, trademarked brand names, song lyrics, misused quotes, etc.; industry standards formatting—following the Chicago Manual of Style and other style books; cohesiveness; continuity; consistency; proper grammar and syntax; scene and chapter transitions; language choice and style; punctuation; stray errors and typos; and formatting or pagination issues.

To continue our previous comparison: your editor ensures your bones have received enough calcium, all vital organs are in place and the muscle and skin has been properly attached in working order.

MEA: A critique partner can cover a portion of those first big picture details but focuses on your previously discussed challenges and his strengths—details you determine before the project has even begun, which we'll discuss in "Chat Four: Preparing for a Critique." It's a rare CP who can look out for all of them, especially at once. We're talking unicorn rare.

JOY: To expect your critique partner to perform these additional tasks is asking too much of his generosity, unless you both have a knack for one or more of these types of edits and agree to trade services.

Book Coaches

MEA: Book coaches are writers more advanced and knowledgeable than you, who you pay to guide you step by step through writing a book. Their work typically occurs in one of three ways. First, a book coach could walk you through the spark of an idea to a place you're comfortable taking the reins or all the way to a finished project.

Second, if you've already begun the project, you could hand him pages you've written, and he can give you insight on why you can't seem to continue. Third, a book coach could take a completed manuscript and flesh out why it's not working, walking you through a revision of your draft.

Your critique partner cannot be a book coach because of the nature of your relationship. You're his partner, and both of you rest on a more even level of experience and expertise. Plus, as we discuss in section three of this chat, your benefits come from both the receiving and giving of critiques.

JOY: Also, all three of these book coach situations constitute a major time commitment, which is fine when that's your job. Being a critique partner is not a full-time job. If you're asking your partner to guide you through each minute step of your project and create action plans for you to complete a work, you're not viewing him as your partner. He's become either your book coach or your editor or both, and you better start paying him in money or fair trade; otherwise, he won't be your "partner" for long.

Grandmothers

MEA: If you're finding only praise-filled comments, you may have accidentally chosen your grandmother as your CP. A beneficial critique partner honestly evaluates your writing without bias. He appreciates your story strengths, laughs with you when you joke and reveres your ability to spin a craft rule. But, he will also point out two-dimensional characters, call you out on plot holes, tell you when things aren't working or when you're mixing your metaphors again. Your grandmother will not do that. She wants to kiss your cheek and feed you pie. This can be a nice respite, but it will not improve your writing.

BULLIES

JOY: A critique partner should genuinely care for you and your progress as an author; so the moment someone attacks you, kick him to the curb, QWERTY Friend. A true partner respects you and your knowledge in the field, or he wouldn't want your critique.

MEA: As an added sidenote: be wary of someone who does not want reciprocation. If you're offered a critique from someone who doesn't have a work in progress, he may not be creatively content. This could tempt him toward sifting your project through an unhealthy screen.

Consciously or subconsciously, this person could belittle you and your project, making you his footstool to reach a fragile personal confidence. He could live vicariously by commandeering your work, overstepping his bounds and injecting his voice on top of yours. This leads to demands rather than suggestions, leaving the term *partnership* far behind, balled up and shaking in the dirt. Without proof of current craft practice and example of his ability, his opinions may be unfounded. Even so, they will still hurt. Words, once spoken or typed—regardless of their truthfulness or validity—cannot be unheard, unread or unfelt.

JOY: At some point in your creative practice, you have likely felt a fragility in your confidence. If so, you know it's more difficult to build belief in your abilities than it is to shatter it. This is one reason we advise discretion in whom you choose to hand unfinished writings and why we will outline in later chats a careful process for you to find the right partner.

Servants

MEA: Requesting too much from your critique partner can slip up on you if you're not on guard. He may even tell you he can take on One. More. Thing. Ideally, though, your critique partner will also be creating. He may have a family, another job, a family member in need of care, a penchant for water sports. The point is, each person is an individual, and you both must have a life outside of writing. Otherwise, what are you writing about?

JOY: Be a guardian for your time and your CP's. Creative people sometimes fill their calendars with promises and self-imposed responsibilities, avoiding their own creative endeavors. Just so you know, we winced at that sentence because we're speaking from personal experiences.

Your need for writerly advice shouldn't be at the forefront of your mind when committing to a partner. You should respect him as a human being as well as a wordsmith, and you may need to voice reason when his fear is all he's listening to. By receiving your help when he's procrastinating, your CP will recognize the signs when he sees them in you. We're not saying don't ask One More Thing; we're saying, before you do, ascertain whether your CP can handle it without forfeiting something important in his life. If you don't, you will be sorely disappointed when your requests rack up, he eventually tells you he can't critique your work anymore and your partnership goes up in flames. Instead, pay attention to verbal and nonverbal cues throughout your partnership and guard his time as you do your own.

WHAT DOES A CRITIQUE PARTNER DO?

MEA: Now that we've addressed some misconceptions, let's outline what a critique partner does. You will likely discover more as you develop your own partnership; but, to start, a critique partner:

- Provides the first sounding board for your work.
- Shares knowledge of writing craft and learns about the medium in which you're writing.
- Gives advice in a way that resonates with you.
- Respects your knowledge and experience as a writer and seriously considers your suggestions on his works.
- Uses his strengths to bolster your weaknesses, while learning from your strengths to grow in his weaknesses.
- And, hopefully, shares ideas and discusses writing joys and woes as your friendship grows.

JOY: For this book's focus, we're not talking about critique groups. While groups like these can mirror a partner relationship, it's a different beast. See Appendix E for our recommendations on surviving group critique situations—such as writing classes or writing group opportunities.

NOW THAT WE'VE HASHED out what critique partners are and are not, it's time for you to discover what you learned. Pull out that shiny new notebook and make three columns: *Misconceptions I Had, CP Facts I'm Most Excited About* and *Questions I Have*.

The purpose of this challenge is to see how much you've already learned. Share this with your critique partner if you already have one. You may discover more common ground. Reference these questions as you read to see which ones we answer.

SECTION II: PURPOSES OF A CRITIQUE PARTNERSHIP

Why Do I Need A Critique In The First Place?

MEA: You—the author—are too close to your story to see its weaknesses. It germinated in your mind and heart, so you know how your characters breathe and think and smell and sound. You know all the whys behind what they do. Will your reader? How will you know without an objective evaluation?

You've internalized all the iterations your story has taken from concept to final draft. The walls of the current story are thin in some areas; and, since we can't all write a book in one sitting, decisions we've made and subsequently unmade seep in. This leads to missteps in everything from setting and plot consistency to theme and character development.

JOY: Embrace that you need an outsider's view. A great critique partner understands your desired results for your story and helps you fix any weaknesses inhibiting that vision.

Outside of story corrections, critiques provide awareness of writing craft weaknesses. Your critique partner may point out repetitive no-nos you should avoid in your next project. This growth leads to a cleaner drafting process with fewer errors in each completed project. You're unlikely to make these discoveries on your own.

MEA: Role-playing time: I'll ask for our skeptical friends, "So what? Why should I pour out so much time and effort into building a writing relationship? Can't I just pay someone to do this and leave me out of the giving end?"

JOY: Actually, yes.

You could hire a developmental editor or a book coach to help you work through your piece, depending on the stage of your project. And, perhaps you still should. Critique partners aren't a way to get rid of the professionals on your team. They simply work as another part of your team. From our experience, the time and effort of a CP relationship are well worth the extensive benefits.

MEA: At the start of our critique journey, we didn't anticipate much beyond "make my book suck less." We evaluated each experience and tailored our process to be most time effective and beneficial, then we uncovered how edifying a critique partner relationship can be. Frankly, the results knocked our socks off.

In case you didn't know, that's a good thing.

FOR THIS CHALLENGE, we want you to journal—just you and the page.

How are you feeling about the idea of a partnership? Do you have past experiences you'd like to get off your chest? Do you have fears or uncertainties about starting a relationship that feels so vulnerable?

This is your journal. Write anything you want. We won't read it. Your dog won't read it. Your cat won't— well, he might; but, let's be honest, he doesn't really care about your emotions. Feel through the ink onto the page. You might be surprised what emerges.

SECTION III: BENEFITS OF A CRITIQUE PARTNERSHIP

What Do I Get Out Of Being Critiqued?

JOY: The old saying "practice makes perfect" fits writers well, but the greatest lessons often arise through a new perspective. After a careful critique from another writer, you will find yourself with an honest view of who you are as an author, a deeper and more well-rounded story and characters or a better-articulated informative work. We become better at our craft by working with other writers. An example of this is finding solutions for suggestions or answering developmental questions posed by your trusted partner. If you can't pinpoint a problem, you don't know it's there. If you don't know it's there, you can't test solutions. If you can't find a solution, you will never grow as an author or gather your readers. You'll leave them unfulfilled and thinking, *Doggone, I wish that book would have been executed better because I really liked the concept.* They will mark you off their reading list; and that is not something you want.

A critique process pushes us to discover our characters' motivations, which may lead to epiphanies about ourselves. Internal insights bring another aspect few writers expect. Critiquing might stir up emotional depths you have left undisturbed. We'll come back to this in Chat Two when we discuss when you're ready for a critique partner.

MEA: Another primary benefit of receiving a critique is learning your natural response to criticism. If you're like us, your work is a piece of your soul; so it's natural to feel anyone who thinks it might need improvement belongs on your personal blacklist. You need to know what to expect your reactions after a critique to look like.

Will your pride puff up and consume you with thoughts like: *He's too simple to understand.* or *Who is he to think he can tell me ...?*

Or, will your self-esteem have a pity party with a gallon of ice cream as the guest of honor while you whimper thoughts like: *I don't know why I even try ....* and *I was stupid to think I could do this ...?*

When a critique comes from someone known and trusted, you can safely navigate the roads of criticism.

JOY: At the end of the day, you should have an advocate and an ally in your CP. The publishing world can be lonely and overwhelming—even brutal. We all need more people in our corners, especially post-publication when critics beat us down. We require the truth and the occasional nudge, but we deserve them from a loving source. Like Mickey was for Rocky in *Rocky III*, our CP can be behind us, screaming in our ear, "Get up! Get up, you *QWERTY edit*, cause Mickey loves ya!"

What Do I Get Out Of Giving Critiques?

MEA: My mom once told me, "If you want to learn something, figure out how to teach it." I believe once you have learned the Thing, finding a way to say it helps others and solidifies that lesson within you. So, what do you get out of critiquing? If you don't know something craft-related, you learn it so you can give a good critique. If you do know something, you articulate it and help your partner learn it while embedding the lesson deeper within your mind.

JOY: This was the most unexpected aspect of critiquing, I think. The more practice you have in identifying rough spots in the written word, the better you are at spotting them in your own writing and implementing improvement. This manifests itself in stronger first drafts and a quicker realization of the rough edges during revisions. When you help your partner clean up his draft, you inadvertently unearth solutions to problems you may have not even made yet. As you embrace this new ability, you eagerly tackle each step in the draft-to-publish process because you've seen the results of each stage's hard work and know how superior that final draft will be.

MEA: You might have read this advice in your search for tips on becoming an author: take your favorite published book and dissect it. The benefit of articulating what you admire and hate is you can see what author story tactics, language, plots and characters resonate with you. You discover inspiration or warnings you can internalize and incorporate into your own writing.

JOY: We bet you're thinking, *Aha! I'll just break down books, articles, short stories and such and not have to talk to someone else. Take that, QWERTYs!*

You could, but that route would only provide half the benefit you could receive through critiquing an unfinished manuscript. The published book has had multiple rounds of revisions and edits, forming it into a product you admire. You're only seeing one side of the work—its best side. You might make a comment that feels profound as you think it.

In truth, it's an assumption as to why the author made a decision that boggled you or felt untrue to the story. You most likely won't have the option to ask the author questions. *Why did you choose ...? What made your character retaliate like that? Why didn't you switch chapter 4 with chapter 16? What's up with the iguana?* Questions like these get unasked; and you can't verify your assumptions.

MEA: This leads to another advantage of breaking down a work in progress. You get to be wrong and be corrected by the author of the piece. When you ask your critique partner questions, he may have some interesting answers. If you discover he meant something different than what you understood, you can work together to help him find a clearer way to develop his vision. If you only make one-sided observations, you might internalize incorrect lessons and never know.

JOY: Further, once you move beyond the "something's not quite right" of evaluating literature, you will begin to grasp the source of the problems. By learning to articulate your theories and suggestions, you'll better understand the *why* of what's wrong with a section. This translates to your work as well as theirs and results in a confidence in the critiquing process.

MEA: Not only that, when you accept invitations to round table discussions or panels with fellow writers, you will already have practice in expressing your thoughts on a topic in a give-and-take manner. You have worked out and strengthened this mental muscle in order to quickly assess and evaluate your colleagues' words and verbalize additional insights.

JOY: I found it encouraging seeing Mea's draft at a stage closer to that of my piece—AKA the "hot mess" stage. This comforted me. Together, we inched our way closer toward publishable products. I'd say it's beneficial to see just how many revisions and how much effort it can take to become someone's favorite author.

MEA: I'd definitely label that a benefit, if not a revelation.

Accountability and community round out our list of assets. Sharing progress and discussing deadlines with each other encourage you to plan your critiquing days which flows to scheduling your writing, and suddenly you're acting like a professional. Beyond that, you develop a sense of pride in each other's works and your partner's accomplishments. You helped his piece to its feet, after all, and most likely will be in the acknowledgments. You have watched your partner grow as an author, supervised the piece from infancy to adulthood and simultaneously grown in your craft area. The more you work together, the stronger your relationship will be and the more joy you'll feel in rising in ranks alongside your partner. This positivity may spread from the two of you as a pay-it-forward boost through your greater literary communities.

Now that we've tucked away some critique partnership benefits, our remaining chats will dive deeper into the *whos, whys* and *hows* of developing and maintaining such a relationship.

QWERTY CHALLENGE

HAVE YOU DISSECTED A published piece you admire or hate to see how it ticks? This exercise reveals what you like and dislike in literature and can give you practice with critique delivery while you're looking for your special literary someone.

You can probably tell we think highly of the whole critique partnership. We're guessing it produces even more benefits than we've shared. What others come to your mind? This is a Challenge we hope you'll return to as you embark on a critique relationship. Drop us a line and let us know what you discover along the way.

Recap

- Defining the critique partnership and what a CP does gives you a common starting point for this topic and for your relationship.
- The opportunity for interactive and collective growth in craft, profession and confidence sets critique partnerships apart from interactions with editors, book coaches or beta readers.
- You're too close to your story, so outside eyes bring a needed objective perspective.
- Deconstructing another piece, pinpointing issues and accomplishments and articulating your findings improve your craft in a time-efficient manner.
- Benefits flow from both giving and receiving literary critiques.

QWERTY CHAT

Evaluating Yourself for Your New Role

CHAT TWO: Evaluating Yourself for Your New Role

WE CHAT ABOUT HOW a writer can know when he's ready to become a critique partner, evaluating himself through three lenses: intellectual, emotional and practical.

SECTION I: INTELLECTUAL PREPARATION

What Self-Knowledge Do I Need to Consider a Critique Partnership?

JOY: We propose establishing a partnership toward the start of your creative journey but not at the very beginning. If you have made the decision to build the foundation for your writing career, your first step is to write. We suggest that fiction authors write short stories in the genres they're interested in to get a feel of story planning and execution. For nonfiction authors, beginning with blog posts or articles on possible topics to write consistently can uncover both voice and niche.

MEA: As much as we think we are experts when it comes to ourselves, we often get it wrong without introspection and experimentation. For example, you need to know your writing strengths and challenges.

You might speculate that your weakness is building three-dimensional characters. Once you finish a few writing projects, you may discover your true weakness is an overuse of exposition that doesn't leave room for your characters to develop.

If you partner with someone who has the same weakness, you both could drown in a pit of flowery language with no plot or character growth providing strong vines for your salvation. Be honest with yourself. Know who you are. Once you do, you're one step closer to being ready to work with a partner.

JOY: Perhaps the best test of when you're ready for a partnership is to review our definition of a critique partner. Candidly answer if you can do and be each of the things outlined there. Only you can answer that, and your honesty is vital for this endeavor to succeed. If you can't commit to living out that full definition, take the steps you need to get there before you move forward. We think you'll be glad you did.

QWERTY CHALLENGE

THIS CHALLENGE HAS TWO PARTS. First, take the time to revisit our QWERTY Definition for a Critique Partner and evaluate your ability to commit to every part. For any problem sections, write out an action plan of what you need to do to embrace it.

> A **CRITIQUE PARTNER** (CP) should be a knowledgeable writer who desires to assist other writers with their works and willingly accepts reciprocation, creating a harmonious relationship that results in literature superior to what the author alone could provide for readers.

Second, if you have written and finished projects, begin a list of challenges you faced for each one. How did you handle them? Were you able to find solutions, or did you find a work-around? What do you think you did well? What questions were you unable to answer? This is the foundation of your strengths and weaknesses evaluation, so keep it handy. We'll revisit it.

What Basic Writing Craft Knowledge Do I Need To Be Helpful?

MEA: In order to analyze someone else's work, a writer needs a basic knowledge of writing craft. You want your fellow writer to have a partner, not a stow-away. Likewise, the more craft items in your intellectual arsenal, the more you can correct in drafting or self-revision before handing over your project, with a clear articulation of where your story is lacking. It is through self-revision that you first hone these abilities.

Ready for a truth bomb? Professionals need answers to concepts they don't know or aren't strong in. Amateurs want someone else to make changes to problems they already know exist because they don't feel like doing it. Kaboom.

JOY: It's true; and the more issues the author addresses on the front end, the deeper the CP's critique can go.

You may wonder why your CP shouldn't just overlook small messes to find deeper issues, so you can make simpler corrections later. Honestly, if you're not willing to fix the little things now, you probably won't fix them later.

Now, consider this analogy: you are looking at an overgrown forest. It's shadowed and crowded. All the

Evaluating Yourself For Your New Role 37

trees appear discolored, and you must walk sideways to follow a zig-zag path through them. You're tasked with testing each tree for disease. Overhead, a clock counts down. How thoroughly can you evaluate each tree under these circumstances? Even though you've been told to ignore the ones with a nonfatal illness, you still must examine each dark spot to determine if it's just a weird shadow cast by neighboring trees or a sign of infection. Sounds daunting, doesn't it?

MEA: On the other hand, envision a healthy forest with properly spaced trees. You scan through and easily locate the diseased trunks—some slight and some considerable—but all in clear contrast to the healthy ones. You take out your tree medical kit and walk from sick tree to sick tree, smiling at the well ones as you pass. The clock ticking above serves as a metronome for bird song instead of a countdown to disaster.

The latter scenario offers a better environment in which to think deeply about proper care for each ill tree within the set time limit. More trees in need of assessment translates to the tree doctor having time only for the initial, more obvious diagnoses—those issues you likely already knew about—instead of a more thorough analysis.

JOY: If you were the evaluator, which scenario would you prefer? An anxious environment where you push through a mess in a vain attempt to reach as many problem trees as possible? Or, would you rather feel the sun's warmth as you pad along soft, mossy grass to thoroughly assess and prescribe care for needy trees?

MEA: Let's take it one step further. How would you feel about the tree farmer who put you in that dense forest? Perhaps you would consider his neglect and subconsciously begin construction on a wall separating him from your trust. That's the beginning of the end.

Moral of the story: don't be lazy. Fix what you know is wrong before handing it off to someone else, so you receive help with the trees you don't know how to treat.

JOY: Practically, what word illnesses should you be looking for? The QWERTYs—that's Mea and me, in case you missed it—have curated a list of extreme basics we feel are essential if you have never, ever critiqued. Most suggestions you give your partner will be filtered through knowledge of these areas. These are at-a-glance explanations.

If the next few concepts stump you, a little more writing craft understanding might be required before you commit to critique. We include a list of QWERTY-approved books and resources in Appendix I to help you garner needed knowledge. We hope our QWERTY Definitions (available all together in the Glossary) provide you a common starting point to share with your new partner as you develop your working relationship.

Genre

QWERTY DEFINITION

GENRE is the label addressing the content of a piece, so people who like to read in a particular field will find it, bookstores will know how to shelve it and digital retailers will know how to list it. For the writer, genre informs him of reader expectations a piece should fulfill. It can guide plot, character motivation and resolution.

MEA: Humans are habitual creatures who tend to want to repeat emotional responses that deliver contentment. Reading exemplifies this desire. For fiction and nonfiction written in narrative formats, examples of emotional responses include the suspense of a mystery, the anticipation of a thriller, the desire of a romance, the wonder of a fantasy, the relatability of a memoir. For informative nonfiction, some reader choices can be guided by emotion but also by intellectual intrigue and the stimulation of learning something new.

Character development and story structure (which we'll get to in a moment) elicit these emotions. If the author doesn't know which genre his piece falls into, it's ideal for him to figure that out before his CP reads a word. The partner can't give his best critique without that information, and his job is made more difficult. On the side of critiquing, you should understand genres in order to alert the author to an error in story choice and to include genre tropes and structures (common storylines and timelines) in your critique process.

JOY: You see, a genre label is a promise to your reader that you're providing a product that satisfies certain expectations. Two of the clearest examples are *cozy mystery* and *sweet romance*. You and your partner want to handle the reader's trust with care. If an author calls his book a *cozy mystery* and chocks it full of blood, guts and gore, his partner better call him on it. The same goes for a *sweet romance* that repeatedly lifts the sheets and lets us know exactly, in explicit detail, what's going on there.

These two examples would require either a rewrite or a simple change of genre. Other times, an author may intentionally choose to alter his story away from genre norms, but he needs to do it excessively well in order for it to fly with readers.

MEA: Genre should be more than a marketing tool, though. If you've not started your piece, we suggest *The Story Grid: What Good Editors Know* by Shawn Coyne as a practical tool to determine your genre and understand it. Honestly, genre choice is one of the first decisions you should make after deciding on which idea you'll focus. Your creativity wants to play, and it thinks it wants total freedom; but, we've found our creativity produces its best work when given boundaries. Solidifying your genre fences by pinpointing the area your creativity can run wild allows its explorations to be usable and on-task. Mostly.

NONFICTION

JOY: Nonfiction writing stands apart from fiction genres because it is varied and specific to the author. This can make it difficult to assess without help on the front end from the author. We highly recommend Joanna Penn's *How to Write Nonfiction* as your best resource for deeper explorations of the types of nonfiction and readers' expectations, should you or your partner write in this area.

For our purposes in this book, we will specify some types of nonfiction critique nuances in Chat Four. Otherwise, you'll find most of our advice transfers between fiction and nonfiction.

What Are The Main Elements Of Story?

MEA: Everything we write tells a story, from epic fantasy sagas to homecare blog posts. Story is what persuades your reader to hang around to the end because they need to know what happens or get all ten tips. We're going to define what we consider the basic bones of story with the disclaimer that you should dive deeper than this book will take you. For vetted resource suggestions, check Appendix I. For now, let's talk about the two foundational elements of any story—character development and story structure.

CHARACTER DEVELOPMENT

QWERTY DEFINITION

CHARACTER DEVELOPMENT is the work an author does to portray a character, whether fictional or real, as true to life through details such as the emotional change from beginning to end, subtleties in personality and internal complexities.

Even nonhuman characters require personification. That's why cartoons make you cry and stories about pets finding their way home make you tense. The writers have applied human emotions and characteristics to their characters.

JOY: Story should have—at an absolute minimum—a protagonist and an antagonist.

> The **PROTAGONIST** is the main character of the story who has a desperate desire for something seemingly out of reach. This should be the character with the most internal change in the story.
>
> The **ANTAGONIST** is the person or thing that hinders your protagonist from getting what he wants, as he simultaneously pursues his own desire.

Without both, there's no conflict. No tension. No plot ... no readers.

MEA: Each of these characters must want something immensely. As each character pursues his desire, their paths collide and threaten to prevent each other from obtaining their individual goals.

Next, the main character needs other blockades to obtaining his goal. Isn't the struggle to prevail against the odds exactly the reason stories resonate with readers? If your partner is unable to identify your protagonist, antagonist, their driving desires and the blockades to those longings, you now know where to begin improving your story.

JOY: Further, your protagonist needs to change over the course of the story. For example, your reader might meet a world-worn, angsty protagonist in Chapter One and follow his journey toward a dissonant and depressed tragic end if you're an Ernest Hemingway-type author. Or, he may work his way to a Pollyanna optimist with a happily ever after if you're a Jane Austen. This is called a character arc.

> A **CHARACTER ARC** is the internal, emotional change of a character from the beginning of a story to its end as a response to trials and circumstances in the character's path.

One of us QWERTYs leans more toward the Hemingway side and one leans more toward Austen. We'll let you guess which is which. The point is, different writers will take varying approaches to how

Evaluating Yourself For Your New Role   45

their characters evolve, but evolve they must or readers you will lose.

Outside of your protagonist, all characters should have at least the shadow of an arc, if you have a character in your story who doesn't change or move the story forward regarding plot or the main character's arc, then you should ask yourself if he's necessary. Critique partners excel in helping one another cut out the lovable but pointless characters.

Speaking of moving the story forward, let's examine our second foundational element.

STORY STRUCTURE

STORY STRUCTURE is the way in which an author chooses to present his tale.

MEA: Once upon a time, Baby Author Mea decided she would write a book. She was young and naïve, so she opened a computer document and typed *Chapter One*, believing her story would appear on the page by the force of want and be whole and perfect when it did. Baby Mea nearly spiraled into a state of depression when she had to loosen her grip on pride's reins and realize the preparation necessary to work a story into existence.

Some think story structure only means if the tale is told chronologically or with an incongruent timeline. That is part of it, yes, but we also think story structure involves all the pieces and parts that should be considered before a project begins. It's a conglomeration of these aspects, done well, that allows readers to end your tale with satisfaction or, at the least, appreciation. Let's define each part now.

QWERTY DEFINITIONS

STORY is a series of struggles and complications concerning real or fictional characters, organized and expressed in a way to elicit a mindset shift or emotional response for a variety of reasons—escapism, curiosity, distraction, morality or persuasion, for example.

PLOT is the ordering of events or happenings in a story that leads to the ultimate resolution and hosts the character arc journey.

PLOT POINTS are main events or happenings that are necessary to character development and plot and act as story guides. Example plot points are exposition (introduction), inciting incident (where the main character is moved to action), climax (intense moment where trouble is faced) and denouement (resolution).

PLOT THREADS link a character to each conflict from the beginning of the piece to the end of it through each plot point. A character can have multiple plot threads.

CONFLICT is created by the obstacles that prevent the characters from getting what they desire.

MOOD is the emotion or emotions evoked in the reader by the story's prose. This aspect is subjective; however, some universal conclusions may be drawn regarding the mood of a piece.

NARRATIVE VOICE is the worldview, cadence and word choice the author uses for the story's narrator.

A STANDALONE is a book in which the story's understanding and resolution is not dependent on another book.

A SERIES is a story told over multiple books or articles that depend on each other for a complete understanding.

JOY: All authors must make these story structure choices. Because these decisions often shift or evolve multiple times between the drafting and publication stages, a CP is an invaluable aid in identifying where consistency is lacking as well as in concocting an action plan to get the work back in shape.

IDENTIFY THE STORY ASPECTS you're uncertain about and take necessary steps to determine why they're tripping you up. Be honest, ask yourself questions and research as needed.

Next, take one of your short stories or articles and find the genre and the basic bones of story as listed in this section. Note if they are deficient or if they're spot on. If you see an inadequacy, practice articulating the issue. Be truthful with your limits. You will never have all the answers and may not even have all the questions, but admitting that is your first step toward incredible growth.

If you haven't written a story or article yet, use a published example for this exercise and then draft your piece to use next.

Section II: Emotional Preparation

What Emotional Preparations Could Increase My Chances For A Successful Critique Partnership?

MEA: You've evaluated your head; next, you should assess your heart. Creativity is personal, as is the work you create. Because of this, you need to know if you harbor emotional tendencies that could keep you from developing trust in this relationship and if, when you receive critical feedback, you can maintain a healthy amount of confidence. Critiques are meant to rip and mend and polish your manuscript into something you're proud of, but not at the expense of your well-being. We believe facing your emotional struggles and taking action to heal or accept them as they come is imperative if you're planning on becoming a career writer. So, the question is, can you do that?

JOY: As creative beings, we tend to live on the emotional side of things. Those emotions come from somewhere, sometimes from a place we recognize and other times from the boundless chasm where repressed feelings, long-overlooked issues, and missing socks go. When we write—especially fiction and narrative nonfiction—we write from our souls. When our work is evaluated, critiqued, revised, edited and reviewed, each of those steps is, in effect, a rending of our souls. We first need to learn to embrace this process of pulling our work apart with the purpose of piecing it back together more polished and perfected. This process should result in satisfaction and the best form of our story. If we can't bear the art of ripping and repairing, though, we'll never view that polished product.

MEA: It goes deeper than merely acknowledging we need help to improve our writing or to see our story from another perspective. If we haven't accepted our past or dealt with our present, when our work is critiqued in the future, it could feel like death by ink poisoning.

Consider the possibility that our story's plot holes and lack of depth spawn from our own emotional state or past experiences. If we find this truth, we can begin to understand ourselves. As we grieve our losses and grasp our hope, we find personal mending an unexpected benefit of our professional endeavors.

It's vital to understand and embrace that a critique could shed light on such personal connections and, therefore, require internal action. Who better to give you that critique than someone you've developed a trust with, who can ease you into this process?

JOY: The action you'll need to take varies by project and emotional issues. When I wrote *Any Good Thing*, my critique partners helped me recognize many of my characters lacked depth and purpose. It wasn't until I wrote the related novella, *Plus One Year More*, that I had my epiphany of why. It turns out, I was oblivious to this lack of depth on my own. With their help, I recognized my shortcoming and went on to discover why it existed. My real-life lack of willingness to open myself up completely to others and my inability to lower the siege-ready defenses I'd spent a lifetime constructing resulted in shallow characters. This personal shortcoming made it difficult for me to write characters who open themselves to others.

My steps came in stages. With the novel, I was able to reevaluate and determine which characters needed larger, more vulnerable roles in my main character's life and how he needed to approach various relationships. That challenge was fairly easy to tackle. It was with the novella where the deeper challenge lay because that story's emotional needs plummeted to the depths of my own issues. I had to push myself deeper and deeper into my own heart and soul in order to heal and understand myself before I could write and revise that story as it deserved.

That's a hard step, but when it's taken and you keep stepping, one foot before the other, magic happens—

healing and a new appreciation for and acceptance of life with all its ups and downs, rights and wrongs, hard and easy. That's probably more than you bargained for when you chose to create, but what a valuable benefit it is. Such emotional growth in the author translates to deeper characters which result in more invested readers who close the back cover changed. That's the power of words.

MEA: Thank you for sharing that, Joy. It's a perfect example.

Now that we understand the far-reaching effects a critique could have, we have three more emotional aspects for you to evaluate.

First, can you embrace this person as a friend and treat him with compassion, forgiveness and grace while giving him respectful truth from a place of love? This empathy allows for gracious acceptance of a critique and patience for the delivery of one.

Second, can you set hubris aside? Will you be open and honest about both your strengths and weaknesses? Will you reward the time your partner put into critiquing your piece by weighing his suggestions without stacking the other side of the scale with your own weights of laziness, pride or stubbornness?

And, finally, can you commit yourself to this other person and his work? Will you care as deeply about his project as you care for your own? Will you be there to push and drive, supporting his efforts to be the best author he can? Will you stay alongside him, cheering as his words find their ways into the hearts of readers?

When you're willing to open yourself up to a critique and whatever depths it may plumb and to nurture this new relationship with honesty, respect and support, we believe you're emotionally prepared to foster a healthy critique partnership.

TAKE AN HONEST LOOK within and conjure the will to search for healing. What is your instinctive response to criticism and commitment? If it's a negative emotion—aversion, distrust, anger, denial, violence—why?

What trauma do you need to understand before engaging in this relationship? What are you afraid of?

We give backstories to our characters and show them how to evolve, but sometimes we forget we're the protagonist in our life's stories. Everyone has a past. It's the imperfect foundation that has made us who we are. We can be so hard-hearted, placing blame on our childhood selves for things outside our control. We may harbor guilt for decisions made before we knew better. This is not a moment of judgement on who you've become but, rather, an opportunity for self-forgiveness.

Likewise, if your past holds pain or trauma, you may be stuck living beneath a shroud. You deserve the chance to feel comfortable in your skin. You're worth the effort to improve your present. Write down your findings. Seeing them on the page might give your thoughts order and provide a new perspective. We challenge you to evaluate yourself and take the steps you need to heal.

Section III: Practical Preparation

Do You Have The Time?

JOY: Let's face it: most writers don't sit around in pajamas all day with no responsibilities beyond creating fictional lands and pontificating upon the philosophical meaning of life.

We're spread thin and run ragged in an attempt to potentially pursue this crazy dream of publication while still paying the bills, keeping the kids and animals fed and maintaining some semblance of a social life. We write in the wee hours of the morning, on the commute to work, in between appointments and whenever we can beg, borrow and steal time and space—even on the back of grocery lists while standing in the checkout line.

MEA: The creation of scan-and-go grocery lines has really cut into my writing time. If you want to know whether you can fit a CP into your life, honestly evaluate your current commitments. Often, taking on a partner will mean shifting priorities or losing an extra obligation. If you decide that having and being a critique partner is valuable and necessary to your growth as a writer, then you will do what's needed. As you and your partner establish a routine, you may find the time needed to devote to each other could lessen or increase. Keep a lookout for ways to optimize your relationship by maintaining an open line of communication.

Should You Have One Or Multiple Critique Partners?

JOY: If one CP is great, ten should be phenomenal, right? Well, we don't have a one-size-fits-all answer, but we do have some suggestions to assist in evaluating what's practical for you.

The first question to ask yourself is, "Do I have the time to reciprocate the assistance I'm hoping to receive?"

MEA: If you either have the time already or are willing to make the time by shifting priorities or evaluating your work schedule, you may want to consider multiple critique partners. Proceed with caution and don't make promises you can't keep, though. If you can only critique two long pieces a year in addition to your life responsibilities, be honest from the start and only promise what you can deliver. Make a schedule to spread big projects throughout the year. Then, keep that schedule. If alterations are necessary, make sure they don't impede on someone else's time without his knowledge and permission. Communication will be your best friend.

JOY: I have multiple CPs and can speak to the benefits of spreading the workload. The main one is the variety of options you'll have. Not all of your critique partners may be available when you need your manuscript evaluated. You're all working on your own projects, too, and often you have deadlines which don't allow for critiquing with every project. We did just suggest scheduling your critiques with your partner(s) as you would a creative project; but, sometimes, inspiration hits or schedules go awry. In these situations, the chances are greater that your piece will receive a critique if you have more than one person to ask.

This happened when I made a somewhat last-minute decision to enter a short story competition in 2018. Two of my four CPs were available. Thanks to their help, my short story won second place and found its home in an incredible anthology.

If all of your CPs are available, you'll receive multiple perspectives on the same piece, which will combine for the betterment of your final product. This is especially handy when it comes to feedback you may not agree with—often either because of pride, an inability to cut what needs to go or a leaning toward the lazy side.

Let's say you have three CPs. One of them says your main character's choice in the second act seems odd. The other two don't mention it. You have two choices here: You can decide that was a personal preference on the part of the one CP and ignore it. Or, if it's making you wonder, ask the other two partners what they think. Reevaluate once you have their responses.

If the majority of your partners agree, they're on to something. On the flip side, if the other two specifically mentioned that decision as a positive in their feedback, you can safely decide it was a good call on your part and keep it as is.

MEA: When you have a little more time before you send off your piece and want opinions at different stages of your own revisions, multiple partners can benefit you greatly. You should know each person's strengths and weaknesses when it comes to providing a critique, so you can ask each one to evaluate certain aspects based on where he shines.

For example, the first critique could focus on big picture plot holes. Once your revisions are done from that critique, you can confirm if those developmental changes worked by sending it to another CP. At that point, you may be ready to focus on some smaller aspects, such as dialogue or scene transitions. Ask your other critique partners to step in and offer their expertise and suggestions.

If something you love is cut by your first critique partner, ask the second partner after he's read your book to read the section as is and as it once was. Request his opinion on which version is best. If the first two partners are split, this is a perfect opportunity to ask the third CP for his thoughts or use your opinion to break the tie.

JOY: Another benefit to multiple partners continues the availability aspect. As you write and revise—and then as you get into writing pitches and blurbs—you may need quick help from someone who's read your manuscript. You can send a message to see who is available at that time. Chances are one of them will be if you have several. This relieves the pressure on them as well. If one is in the middle of his own work and cannot spare the time, he shouldn't feel guilty for declining your request.

Finally, we must caution this is not a the-more-the-merrier scenario. We hold to the idea that one to four partners is the CP safe zone. More than that and you may be overwhelmed with suggestions on your project and with your time eaten up by other people's dreams.

KEEP A TIME JOURNAL. Document moments of your day for ten days to a full month. Be honest and real. If you spent an hour and change eating ice cream and listening to the new Billie Eilish album, own it. Lying to yourself only keeps you where you are. See where you can and can't alter the things you do in a day to make time for your writing, revising and critiquing.

If you aren't keeping a planner, do so. Immediately. We are shocked that you've made it this far in life without one. (We like planners and schedules and all things organizational.) You can fashion a notebook to your specific needs or find a premade one or go digital.

However you do it, you need to keep up with your responsibilities; you do a lot more than you think. When you make writing an inked-in priority, you're more likely to honor the commitment and complete a project.

Do you not have the time you'd like? You can look into time-saving practices, like time-blocking (see Joy's post in Appendix G) or focusing on one project at a time rather than hopping from one to another. Once you've sucked out every minute you can, decide if you can successfully juggle one or more critique partners at this point in your writing life. If you can't right now, reevaluate next year. Things could change.

Recap

- You need to know your writing strengths and weaknesses before seeking out a critique partner.
- Prepare for a critique partnership by solidifying your basic writing craft knowledge. Our definitions of these tools provide a common place to start as you gain hands-on experience with each.
- Accepting that our writing is connected to who we are—and perhaps who we have been—and understanding that critiques will initially sting will help you decide if you're emotionally ready to initiate a critique partnership.
- Honestly evaluating your daily responsibilities will reveal if this is the right season for you to secure one or multiple critique partners.

QWERTY CHAT
Choosing a Critique Partner

CHAT THREE: Choosing a Critique Partner

OUR PARTNERSHIP STEMS FROM part luck, part hard work and full commitment. In this chat, we share ways you can seek out your own partner and build your relationship on a solid foundation or strengthen the partnership you already have.

Section I: Know Your Author Self

What Is Your Writing Purpose and Process?

MEA: Choosing the best partner begins with knowledge of your literary goals and process so you can swap this information with one another. You're looking for commonalities with enough differences to make life interesting. No matter your personal answers to the following questions, being up front with your potential CP is best practice.

Take the time you need to determine what you want from and for this writing life. It's a hard, bumpy path, and you need commitment as much as you need to be committed. You want a CP who has the same ultimate desires as you, so you can move in parallel directions instead of gradually separating ones.

When publication is your goal, you'll want to share how you plan to achieve that—traditional, Indie or hybrid. For more information on what each of these paths to publication mean, our list of recommended resources in Appendix I has you covered.

You may want to give your story away on a blog or share site or only to family. That's so wonderful—a treasure, for sure. But your CP needs to understand your goals from the beginning.

JOY: Beyond the practicality of what you plan to do with your writing once it's done, you should seriously contemplate why you write in the first place. What's your writing purpose, Friend? Why do you have to pick up that pen or fire up that computer? What is it about writing that satisfies you like nothing else? Write down your answers to these questions and keep them handy. You'll need them on the hard days. Trust us. We know.

Why do you need to start here? Well, how are you going to make sure you're choosing the right critique partner if you can't even tell him what you write, why you're writing it, who you're writing for, how you want to write it or what you want to do with it once written?

MEA: You can't communicate if you don't know your message and without communication you can't confidently choose a CP or begin a lasting relationship.

Next comes exploring and examining the kinds of writing you enjoy. If you've been writing short fiction as we suggested, you'll have a leg up here. You can also begin the process of finding your writing style.

How Do You Find Your Writing Style?

Search for answers to questions about your writing, its audience and purpose, through your own short fiction or nonfiction, blog articles or journaling. The beauty of exploration with shorter writing is you learn quickly because you achieve a completed piece faster. You can then revise, self-edit and further examine the piece in a timely manner to help you answer those introspective questions.

JOY: That leads to our second author self-knowledge point—your process.

Shorter pieces allow a more rapid run-through of the writing process—an experience you need in order to be a critique partner. Serious writing doesn't end with a first draft. When you type *The End*, you've reached the beginning. You need to read what you've written and begin self-revision and self-editing.

The same short pieces that teach you your strengths and weaknesses as a writer will be perfect for learning to revise and edit, so have those on hand for upcoming challenges.

MEA: Learning your writing, revision and editing processes will also take research outside of your own writing. Read about other authors' processes, check out library books on the writing craft, ask other writers what they do. Then—and this is key—try the ideas that stand out. Combine suggestions, strip others down, make something new. You may find you prefer a four-column story board combined with monomyth plot points (also called the Hero's Journey, a structure developed by Joseph Campbell), or you may decide loose outlining saves your bacon when it comes to productivity.

JOY: Because all creatives are individuals, no two processes will be exactly the same. Don't get stuck in the web of draft-revise-and-produce-your-book-this-way-and-no-other-way. Read about various methods, try new things and keep layering your process until it becomes your own. The only way to do this is through trial and error, so get ready to fail so you can learn how to succeed your way.

IN ORDER TO UNDERSTAND the kind of partner you should look for, you must first gather your author information to share. To do this, we have a few exercises for you throughout this chat. These challenges will take time. We promise the work you put into them will be worth it, though. We'll be right here, waiting; and so will your next step!

You can probably guess what we're about to ask you to do. Grab your notebook and journal your answers for the following questions:
- What do I plan to do with my writing?
- Why do I have to write?
- What do I want to write? Why?
- Who am I writing for?
- What are key elements of my writing process? (Bonus points for knowing bits about your revision and editing processes.)

What Are Your Strengths And Weaknesses?

MEA: You began a strengths-and-weaknesses list in Chat Two, so you're probably wondering when that gem will come back up.

How about now?

Let's expand on that list so you know what help you can offer your future CP and what to ask him to do for your writing.

The QWERTY recommendation to analyze your strengths and weaknesses is to gather short pieces that have been shelved between a week and a month. When you pull out the first sample to revise, look at it as a piece written by someone else. What do you like about it? Where does it fall short? What lines stand out to you? Why? What do you wish the author would have done? Write out your answers so you can articulate them to yourself and to your new CP. Do this again three to five times. Repetition is necessary because you can't isolate a pattern if you haven't evaluated multiple pieces.

If you need time to write and shelve these pieces, you can outline the writing process aspects that work — or don't — during production. Lessons arise in every step.

JOY: Once you've made it through several rounds of revisions, reflect and answer a few more questions. In what areas could you use practice? Do you struggle when it comes to bringing out a clear theme? Does charting a character's arc make your eyes glaze over? Are you still confused about the difference between plot and conflict?

It's okay. Every writer has specialties and challenges. You'll immediately be a better reviser, self-editor and writer just by acknowledging which aspects of writing are your good, bad and uglies. Once you've identified your strengths and weaknesses, you can share exactly what you bring to the critiquing table and what help you need from a partner.

ARE YOU STILL UNSURE how to develop your magic strengths and weaknesses list? That's okay! We will take the process one step at a time in this Challenge.

Step 1: Take between three and five pieces you've written and note where you're proud and where you would like to improve. False modesty or inflated ego have no place in this exercise. In order for this to work and for you to grow, you must be level-headed and unbiased. We believe this process works best when you haven't looked at the piece in at least a week. Evaluating more than one piece helps you pinpoint patterns in your writing and gives you tangible proof of your abilities. Solidify your list of strengths with specific details you believe you did well. Likewise, make your list of weaknesses based on proof of the areas you would like to improve. We have the tendency to be mean to ourselves, often unnecessarily. Providing proof either way will help you stay honest to yourself and enable you to produce an accurate list.

Step 2: Take several pieces you didn't write but admire. Write down why you love them and what brings you back to them. Is it the words, the characters, the descriptions, the dialogue, the pacing? Be specific and include excerpts from the text for you to return to in the future. Evaluate if you are implementing some of these things you appreciate in your own writing. These can go under your strengths column if you feel proud of your application. Next, pinpoint the things you'd like to do but are unsure how to or have tried unsuccessfully. Those go under the challenge or weakness column. Now we have goals to reach. We QWERTYs love a good goal!

Step 3: If you've had feedback on anything you've written, now is the time to compile it. These aspects belong on your lists as well if you find supporting proof in your work. If you've had unsubstantiated negative feedback—not solid constructive criticism—weigh it against the evaluations you've done for yourself. If it doesn't add up and you can't find textual proof of their opinions, you know you can logically discount those thoughtless words, leaving them behind as you step toward your writing future.

Through this three-step process, you might discover something you thought was a strength is not. Maybe you think you're a master at dialogue, but you're repeatedly given dialogue pointers. Perhaps you should revisit your dialogue with an open mind and willingness to improve if needed. Likewise, a perceived weakness may be a strength at this point, thanks to your focused attention. You have a strength you can now use to assist another writer. How exciting is that?

All legitimate suggestions can aid you in finalizing your list of strengths and weaknesses. Take a moment to celebrate how far you've already come! Now you're ready to move forward with a game plan of what you know and what you need help improving in your writing.

What Is Your Critique Style?

MEA: As you completed the last challenge, you developed revision and critique skills. Take some time to reflect on those revisions. What story improvements did you gravitate toward? Are you best at finding ways to deepen characters? Do you thrive on improving pacing? Do you have an eagle eye for inconsistencies and plot holes?

JOY: Do you pour everything you've got into a critique—to the point you clog up the track changes margins and cause your word processing program to implode? Or, do you give succinct matter-of-fact critiques with the bare minimum of marks and one summarizing assessment at the end? You may prefer periodic paragraph responses within the document or real-time notes as you read. Knowing how you naturally give critiques enables candid discussions with your potential or current critique partner regarding his needs as well.

EVALUATE HOW YOU TEND to provide feedback, even if your only experience is to yourself. Examine self-revisions or previous critiques. Do you get right to the point or do you seek ways to add two positives to every criticism? Writing out what you discover about your choices will assist during the interview process with potential CPs. If you don't provide critiques the way someone needs to receive them, it's best to know before you commit.

What Critique Presentation Needs Do You Have?

MEA: If you don't know which critique type works best for you, don't worry. We have a way to practice with a potential CP, which we'll address further in Chat Four. We have found that, in general, people want to receive the kind of critique they instinctively give out. This could be a starting point for you. We also encourage you to keep an open mind if your partner suggests other ways to give and receive critiques. Be adaptable, but if something new doesn't sit well, be honest and find what does work.

JOY: As you progress together, your partner will need to know if you require your feedback accompanied by questions and easing phrases like, "Could it be that …?" or "I think that maybe …." Be honest with him and yourself. We all need constructive criticism that will help us and our stories improve, but if you need it presented in a gentle manner, don't be afraid to ask. If you prefer blunt, to-the-point feedback where you don't have to wade through niceties, make that clear. Either way, you need a critique that sets you up for a successful revision; and, if you've chosen your partner well, he wants to provide you with that.

MEA: If you're unsure what type of comments will help you most, think back on the times you've been given advice that inspired you to improve. Analyze why that advice at that moment was the thing you needed to hear. This is a great place to start when advising your partner on how to share suggestions with you. You can't expect him to mysteriously know what you need or what you're thinking. Commit to spelling out the details once you know something is right or wrong.

DECIDE WHAT STYLE OF critique presentation you prefer—concise and candid, detailed with extensive examples, constructive criticism padded with positives or something else. If you've previously received critiques—good or bad—reflect on those. What helped you improve? What sent you to the corner, rocking in the fetal position? Write out these reactions in a cohesive manner you can share with potential CPs.

What Are Your Author Personality, Craft Quirks And Craft Preferences?

JOY: Other personality and craft specifics to understand in order to discuss with your potential or current critique partner include writing style and genre preferences; worldview, past trauma and memories; writing goals and the drive to achieve them.

WRITING STYLE AND GENRE PREFERENCES

Sometimes, people are weird. The list of things they can and can't tolerate may be even more weird. If a preferred writing style or genre preference is on your weird list, share your strangeness with your critique partner. This information will most likely affect your evaluation and the amount of support you can offer. If you have intense feelings for or against a particular point of view, for instance, that could determine whether or not you can objectively evaluate a work in that style. If first person stories make you want to rip your hair out, you need to be upfront with that information and probably shouldn't critique a book written that way.

It's the same with genre preferences or aversions. If horror stories upset your mental state, you shouldn't entertain the idea of critiquing for a person who primarily writes horror.

MEA: However, if you're unfamiliar with a genre but you're willing to read something out of your comfort zone with an open mind, focusing on the aspects of story and genre tropes you understand, tell your partner. Explain your lack of experience with the genre and let him decide if he wants you to continue. He will respect your honesty.

For example, Joy wrote a literary fiction novel. As her critique partner, I had to be honest and express that my habitual reading genres are women's fiction and magical realism. Through previous conversations and critiquing projects, Joy knew I have an appreciation for all literature—no matter the genre.

JOY: I also know Mea has a familiarity with developmental editing. I felt confident she would treat my book with respect and offer a viewpoint I would need to take the manuscript to the next peak. I had the option to say "I'll catch you next time" and ask another writer to critique my project. Of course, sometimes it eases your mind to know your book baby will be handled with care because it's in the hands of someone who cares for you and your emotional well-being.

MEA: How can you know what genres you like and style aspects you prefer? You read. A whole lot. Think back on the fiction and nonfiction pieces you love and break down why you love them. Is it the characters? The setting? The lyrical language? The pacing and plot?

JOY: What are you currently reading? Are you loving it? Why or why not? Think as a writer on the craft level and pick apart the piece. What books do you naturally steer away from? Is your aversion based on personal experience or assumptions? What book descriptions draw you in? What do you automatically buy no matter what's on the back cover? Analyzing your current reading habits and pinpointing why you love and hate what you do will provide you with a helpful list of writing style preferences and biases.

You need to share upfront if you will not read certain genres or content for reasons of religion, personal conviction or traumatic experiences. The ultimate goal for critique partners is to become a team for the long haul. If you can't be on board with assisting in each other's goals, why pour your time and effort into building a firm foundation and learning to work with one another? No one will be mad with your honesty. Ultimately, you save your potential CP time and effort, too.

MEA: The next big question is this: can you set aside your biases, read whatever your partner is writing and give it an honest craft-centered critique without procrastinating, missing deadlines or injuring yourself internally or externally? You owe it to yourself and to your partner to give a candid answer. If you can't commit yourself 100 percent to the critique, tell your partner and let him decide if you are still a good fit for his piece or not.

WORLDVIEW, TRAUMA AND MEMORIES

JOY: Deeper than writing style or genre preferences, every person has a worldview—a way through which he filters the happenings he directly or indirectly experiences. A person's belief system, past experiences, understanding of right and wrong and codes of ethics and morality drive his worldview. Each reader brings his worldview into whatever he's reading. It influences the way he understands what he reads and his takeaways after the last word is consumed.

Worldview often affects a critique. For example, someone who believes in an afterlife full of hope and promise may have a hard time objectively reacting to a book where the main character dies without that hope.

A person with a past tainted by patriarchal abuse may be unable to focus on the needed critique points in a book where a character and his father have a close bond. He can't fathom a healthy parental relationship and keeps waiting for the other shoe to drop. When that falling out doesn't happen, this person feels discontent as a reader and may note that as a fault in your piece. If you know his aversion to father/child relationships before, you may be able to overlook his comments degrading the relationship. However, you should have made your partner aware of what he was about to face and given him an option out.

Honestly evaluate yourself in areas of unease to determine if you can objectively critique certain topics. If not, simply walk away. Your partner is your friend. He will understand; and, if he doesn't, you probably needed to reevaluate your relationship anyway.

MEA: You don't have to scrap the idea of critiquing a piece because of trauma. For example, Joy's novel included descriptions of a traumatic circumstance with which I had first-hand experience. Joy gave me the option of receiving the project in full or with the detailed narrative surrounding that circumstance removed. I chose the edited version because that was the best option for my mental health. A compromise, sure, but it was the right choice as repercussions of that experience continued to unfold. I appreciated the option to avoid the "hard stuff" and still help Joy better her piece. It made me feel like maybe this circumstance didn't have to overtake everything I held dear.

> Be respectful of your partner's circumstances or past and allow him to make the decision to either face sensitive topics in a manuscript or work around them. Don't make decisions for your critique partner. Allow him the dignity of choosing.

JOY: Some people have emotionally taxing aversions to certain things that may be uncommon and wouldn't be something an author would consider including in a list of "trigger subjects." This is why it's important to really know yourself when considering scenarios that could be difficult—or even impossible—to critique.

One further possibility a team could encounter is that one partner has suppressed some traumatic memory to the point that he doesn't even know to mention it. Reading about that issue could open the floodgates on a buried past. If such an extreme situation were to happen, the reader should not blame the writer. Likewise, the author should lovingly release his partner from any critiquing expectations. He can then become a support for the friend who just unearthed a land mine he must defuse.

We realize we're examining extremes, but we believe it's important to understand that literature is powerful. Words have birthed societies; they've also crushed kingdoms. With this appreciation for the power of words in mind, we chose to give thoroughness to this topic. If you're a widely-read person, chances are you have faced unexpected emotions through reading at some point already. In this step of self-evaluation, thoroughly consider anything that could cause you emotional distress. March ahead with a mutual understanding that you have each prepared as much as possible for any scenario and are committed to empathy and understanding just in case.

MEA: Human nature sifts everything we say, do and think through the screens of our past, which include positive and negative memories. We have conscious and subconscious feelings about certain people, places, situations and philosophies because of life experiences. Art at its heart impresses upon the artist the need for revelation and healing. Writing, as an art form, is no different.

Whether writing or critiquing fiction or nonfiction, words can reveal areas we need to reflect upon. They can, in turn, help locate the wound so care and healing can begin. One reason critiquing requires great care is, sometimes, both author and critique partner are bleeding and bandaging on the page.

It can be harmful to the author and the relationship if that author doesn't know his partner has negative feelings toward a particular thing in the manuscript. And, the one critiquing may not even recognize he's using prejudices and unforgiven ill will to hinder his partner.

As a critique partner, you will need to train yourself to recognize, alter, extract and issue a disclaimer for personal biases or preferences or from past experiences that leaked into your feedback.

JOY: How about a lighter example? Let's say you were attacked by a rogue squirrel during your eighth-grade picnic. Your loathing, embarrassment and fear may render you unable to see the beauty and careful crafting in the writer's plot twist to transform a villain-assassin-squirrel into a savior.

Before you angrily type a comment resembling, "Lies! Impossible! Not enough willing suspension of disbelief on the planet!" step away from your emotions and attempt to separate yourself from the image of that horrific incident. Replace the squirrel in your imagination with a butterfly or something you love and reconsider the transformative scene.

If you still can't shake the image of the squirrel attack, be honest with the writer. Express your concerns, but present them along with your personal bias. "Lies! Impossible! Not enough willing suspension of disbelief on the planet! By the way, I was attacked by a squirrel when I was young, and this comment may contain residual emotions from that experience."

On the other side, perhaps you adore dragons. They have been your favorite creature your entire life. When you were young, you imagined one came to you and offered his help if things got rough. You haven't used your trump card to call the lovely beast yet, but it's a comforting presence in times of trouble. Can you objectively see the problem when a dragon character's dialogue in your partner's piece sounds cheesy and forced or when his roles read flat and stereotypical?

MEA: Squirrel attacks and lovable dragons aside, recognizing where you tend to lean toward a particular judgement and noting that for your CP will give you a more honest and helpful critique.

What If You Can't Overcome Your Personal Bias Or Preferences?

JOY: Some things stick with you even after all your work to overcome. If something is still preventing you from separating your biases or preferences from an objective critique, you've got to admit that to yourself and respect your partner by bowing out of the possible critique relationship gracefully. Explain your issues in the proper "It's-not-you-it's-me" conversation.

Make sure he doesn't believe you're simply abandoning him or that there's something wrong with his writing. If you must part ways with a critique partner, an honest explanation would make it something other than defeat.

If his story triggers a particularly painful part of your past, we are not saying you need to spill your guts or explain your history. We do urge you to be intentional in your explanation to let him know the story raised some personal issues you need to handle, but your departure has nothing to do with him, his writing or his gummy bear collection.

MEA: Hopefully, your partner will understand, and you can find other ways to support each other in future writing endeavors. We also encourage you to reach out to someone who can help you walk through this personal valley. Counselors can, quite honestly, change your future by assisting you in overcoming your past. Get the help you deserve, Friend!

GOALS

JOY: Finally, you've got to be clear on your writing goals and the determination you have to achieve them. If you have planned out your next ten years and set big picture goals, medium goals and small goals in order to achieve all the big dreams you've envisioned, you need to find someone equally driven. Otherwise, you're headed for frustration.

If you're a planner and you team up with someone who flies by the seat of his pants, doesn't set goals and isn't consistent in working toward completion of projects, yours is a doomed partnership. Likewise, if you plan to write multiple full-length books every year, you need to make sure a potential partner is available for that work load. If the other partner completes one piece every three years, he may end up frustrated that he is critiquing more work than he's having reciprocated.

MEA: Want some tips on setting goals? Whether you're a goal-master or think we're talking soccer, head to Appendix H for "Joy's Case for Goals."

QWERTY CHALLENGE

MAKE A LIST OF your writing style and genre preferences to share with your critique partner and to return to often. We've made a template for you.

Fill in the following or copy it into your journal. These preferences will likely adjust as you change and grow as a writer. Your honesty in filling in this chart will serve you well. Even if you feel silly expressing a loathing for first person point of view, if you don't admit it now and end up with a CP who writes exclusively in first person, you're in for a rocky road ahead.

	PREFERRED	DREADED/HATED/NAILS-ON-A-CHALKBOARD
POINT(S) OF VIEW		
TENSE(S)		
GENRE(S)		

Next, take time to reflect through journaling. What is your worldview? How could it affect your ability to critique? Have you ever had aversions to literature because of your beliefs or convictions, memories or other experiences? Explore that here. We encourage you to consider any trauma in your past and potential triggers (e.g., suicide, abuse, war). As life continues to unfold, you will likely need to update this list from time to time.

Finally, write out your goals. Decide where you want to see yourself in one year, five, a dozen. Write down how many writing projects you plan to work on in a year. Determine how committed you are to making each of these happen. If you need help with writing strong goals, see the article in Appendix H for tips.

SECTION II: KNOW YOUR POTENTIAL PARTNER

Where Can You Find A Critique Partner?

JOY: Finding any companion is hard, and you're going to have to be persistent. You may be starting with a few people in mind or have invested years with a CP and want to make the partnership deeper. Regardless of the point from which you're starting, you're embarking on a process. We believe the results will be worth your emotional output.

You may have noticed, through the self-evaluation portion of finding a critique partner, how important it is to find someone who is compatible. However, compatible doesn't mean matchy-matchy. Strengths and weaknesses between partners should complement. A similar workload, approach and set of values between partners could be helpful as well, but it won't do much good if you both excel and struggle with the exact same things. The non-negotiables, though, are each partner must commit to honesty, communication and a reciprocal partnership.

MEA: This is all well and good on paper, but how do you find this writerly unicorn? In the two worlds we live—the natural world and the cyber world—both require the same friend-making skills. Go in search of someone outside your comfort zone. A significant number of writers are completely comfortable seeing people on holidays only. If you're going to find a critique partner who will elevate your writing, you have to—we're sorry to say—socialize. In the natural world—that's the one you walk around in—just living life can present you with possible critique partners. Look around for people who are writing in your classroom, the library, writers' groups and book clubs. Be brave and talk. Ask the person next to you at the library who's also typing away, if he writes stories. He may only be updating his social media, or he could be crafting a novel, an article, an essay—one that you could help with.

He may like the same television shows and book genres as you; he may even write in the same field as you and have the same ultimate goals. Isn't that exciting? To potentially have someone who you can share enthusiasm with when you think of the perfect resolution to your story's main problem, isn't that the dream? To have a person to brainstorm plot holes with who can add dimension to your characters, isn't that the goal?

JOY: I attended an author event at my local library and pushed past my anxiety to introduce myself to someone. It turns out, we're neighbors with debut books that launched within a few months of each other. Now, we can walk down the street to share a cup of tea and our creative endeavors. You never know what a smile and simple "Hello!" can lead to in your life.

MEA: You will exert a lot of emotional energy by placing yourself in vulnerable positions, but we grow by pushing ourselves. Pencil in time to recover from the stress and then go out again.

You may find it less intimidating to look online for your critique partner. We completely understand. If this is you, seek out digital locations similar to the in-person ones we referenced. Are you in online classes? Email someone whose discussion answers you like. Online book clubs, writing group forums and social media groups provide opportunities to make initial contacts. Seek digital events, critique partner hangouts and social media chats. Sometimes the answer falls in your lap, but more often, it takes asking the question out loud or in type for someone to respond. We included some QWERTY-vetted online forums for you in Appendix I.

JOY: As you do this, the mamas in us must remind you to be vigilant. Look out for creepers. Trust your instincts and walk away if anything feels wrong. Online or in person, be brave but cautious.

Set up precautions to stay safe. Observe how the person you're considering interacts with others in the digital sphere or in his life. If your gut is telling you to move on, it's probably right. Set up a new email address you can cancel if anything gets weird. Don't give out too much personal information until you can trust the person. If you're meeting in person, do so in a public place, like a coffee shop or restaurant without servers. (Please don't hold up a table and stunt a server's tips for the night. The QWERTYs stand for the responsibility to support your servers!)

MEA: If you're getting a creeper vibe, make sure the person doesn't follow you home. We believe it's wise to hope for the best and prepare for the worst. If your caution is unwarranted, good. The ideal is your safety without worry. But, we're realists so we suggest you practice caution until you feel safe … plus a little longer.

JOY: One final word of caution for you: don't be too hasty to offer your help. Mea and I are natural people pleasers, so we have to consciously practice restraint to not offer help on every post we see in our various online writing groups. Sure, we should all be helpful and seek to give more than we ask; but we also have to remember we've only got so many hours in a day and so much mental bandwidth to go around. Help when possible. Remain silent and observe other times.

If someone strikes you as a person with whom you have much in common and whose work you could champion, it will become clearer once you've interacted for a while before you commit. When we commit to being genuine online, it will show; just as the opposite does. "Truth will out," as the old saying goes!

QWERTY CHALLENGE

MAKE A LIST OF possible CPs you already know or of the places you could search for a CP—online or in your community. For online groups or CP-specific forums, check out the QWERTY recommendations in Appendix I. Put your list in the order of your interest at this point. Now, keep that list close. You'll be using it soon!

How Should You Get To Know A Potential Critique Partner?

MEA: Now that we've established where to find potential CPs, we're going to jump to what you need to know about them. Don't worry! We're going to give you all the hows of moving from finding to knowing to keeping a CP. As partners, you'll work together closely on the work of your heart, so you need to get to know one another on both professional and personal levels.

To do this, we have developed a comprehensive interview sheet for you and any potential CPs to complete. You will find it in Appendix C. Use it as is, add to it or simply let it be a template for your own. This interview can be helpful at any stage. If you're in an established partnership, try it out with your current CP, whether you've been together a month or ten years. Before we cut you loose to answer all the questions, let's examine some of the information this interview will produce and why it's important for a critique partnership.

Professional

BACKGROUNDS AND EXPERIENCE

JOY: You will want to know his professional background and any experience that may be beneficial to your writing relationship. Just because a writer doesn't have a background in journalism or creative writing or a similar field doesn't mean he can't be a fantastic critique partner. You may find yourself writing a dystopian Sci-Fi thriller, and your CP's background in microbiology can give you incredible insights into how to accurately create a fictional super strain of virus. On the flip side, if you have extensive writing experience and your CP just began writing creatively last year, you will need to evaluate if his abilities and your needs are a fair match.

Goals

MEA: Discuss your writing goals as well. Make sure you both desire to improve your writing skills for the same purpose—publication or readership.

When your goal is publication, that comes with another set of possibilities. Do you plan to seek an agent with the desire to shoot for the Big 5? Would you rather query directly to smaller or regional presses? Are you more interested in publishers with specific interests, such as religious companies? Do you plan, instead, to publish yourself?

Carefully consider these factors when evaluating another person's work. What is important in seeking representation to approach top publishing companies differs greatly from the focus of an Indie Author. Some types of companies require certain expectations to be met and content guidelines to be followed. The author must know this, but he also needs to share this information with his potential critique partners.

From this discussion, you may find common bonds or be able to share information on publishing options or submission procedures and continue your partnership into another stage of the author's journey.

STRENGTHS AND WEAKNESSES

JOY: Your potential partner should follow the same three steps you did to uncover his strengths and weaknesses. Hand him that previous challenge, also available in Appendix B. If he comes back to you with a list of strengths and no weaknesses, run for the mountain peak. He is dishonest and maybe a tad narcissistic.

If he presents you with only weaknesses, he needs to work on his confidence before understanding the give and take that comes with a critique. If he gives you a balanced list and you can tell he's spent time on each point, you can rest assured he is taking this seriously. That's a huge point in his favor.

Now that you each have your lists, you can see how you might balance one another. If you have all the same weaknesses, it may be that you can't help one another like you originally thought. You could, however, improve those areas together. Two heads are better than one when it comes to learning craft. Share what you've each learned and become study buddies. You may grow into critique partners one day.

MEA: We want to be clear. Based on our experience, the most beneficial critique partnerships pair writers whose strengths and weaknesses complement one another; however, this is not the only approach. If you find a partner whose columns look eerily similar to yours, but you're both willing to learn and grow, building one another up through research and study of the craft, then go for it. As with most aspects of the writing endeavor, there are very few set-in-stone *musts*.

You will discover that, even though you have the same strengths, he'll still have a different perspective on it than you and will be a new, unbiased pair of eyes for evaluation. Likewise, when you both struggle in the same areas, you can work together to research, each taking a different approach and sharing whatever you learn. Talk about an efficient learning style!

With his list of strengths in hand if you choose him as a CP, you can determine what to ask for in a critique. If you choose to have multiple partners, their lists can help you decide who to give your manuscript to first or may influence the questions you ask each one to address during his evaluation. You'll have clear expectations of what he can and cannot deliver.

JOY: Whether your abilities match up perfectly or line up complementarily, we encourage you to find someone at an equal level of craft understanding with a similar work ethic and drive.

QWERTY TIP

Remember, a critique partner at the same level as you means you can more equally give to one another as you grow from and with each other.

In a few years, you should be stronger writers with new strengths and new challenges. These exercises are valuable to revisit every few years for that reason. Don't forget to congratulate yourselves on how far you have come as you reevaluate your good, bad and uglies to determine what to focus on next.

PERSONAL

MEA: Once you've determined you're a professional match, you can take it up a notch. Get to know one another on a personal level. Even seemingly trivial details—like favorite shows or hobbies—can strengthen your professional relationship by giving you a common bond to relate to or an analogy to pull from when trying to explain a critique suggestion.

JOY: We're partial to *Firefly*.

MEA: Shiny!

To build a true friendship, you should connect on levels outside of writing. Some people would rather maintain a strictly professional working relationship with a critique partner, and that's fine too; as long as you're both clear about that and mutually agree that's the type of partnership you're looking for. Our personal relationship has aided us in knowing what triggers to alert one another to in a manuscript or by understanding why one of us is struggling in writing a scene—sometimes before the author does.

Either way, certain aspects you uncovered during the examination of your personality quirks and preferences will spill over into your professional relationship because this is not just a professional partnership, it's a creative one. As such, our worldview and emotional considerations and past traumas must be acknowledged because, even if we don't say them out loud, our work will eventually reveal them.

How This Applies To An Actual Critique

JOY: And now, the main event—getting to know his critiquing abilities. After you discuss your professional backgrounds, goals, needs and individual skills, as well as the personal mindsets and preferences that drive you, it's time to hand each other a short story, article or the first one to ten pages of a more lengthy project. He will then critique yours, and you will critique his.

Why after the interview? Why the additional step? Can't we just call each other partner and get on with it? you might ask.

You need to know if your potential critique partner can adapt his suggestions based on your desires for the project. Alternatively, it's your responsibility to provide him with the information to tailor the critique to your needs.

A CP should be given boundaries and specifications, or he will perform a critique under assumptions that could be outside of your needs. The only way to know if you can work together is … to work together.

MEA: We chose a length limit because if you two don't mesh, neither one of you need to waste more time than necessary. In this process, though, we suggest you trust your instincts and compare them with the facts. If everything looks good with the interview and compatibility, but you feel the critique is lacking and your gut is telling you to run, maybe you should.

What you're looking for in a trial critique are golden nuggets that create thoughts like, *I didn't think of it that way.* or *That's really interesting.* or even *I can't believe I didn't catch that before!* Your partner should be different enough from you to offer a perspective you haven't noticed in your writing.

JOY: When the interview, the critique and your instinct match up, we feel like you have a solid foundation and may have found your Person.

IT'S TIME, FRIEND!

Head to Appendix C for the interview questions. If you haven't already, fill in your own answers. Take your time and make sure your answers are thorough and candid. Utilize the Strengths and Weaknesses Challenge as well; you can find that in Appendix B. If you match up equally or complementary as desired, you're ready for a sample critique. You will find important details on the types of critiques in Chat Four.

Once you're ready, get to know your potential partner in order to set up a foundation strong enough to build a full kingdom for your futures. To do this, you must first know yourself, then you should put in the time to get to know him, using the tools we've provided.

Finding a critique partner takes bravery and caution, but the best things are found on the other side of fear.

Check out Mea's Theory of Fear in Appendix F for further examination of the topic.

Recap

- Knowing what you want to do with your writing and why you write, your strengths and weaknesses, your critique style, your critique needs, your literary preferences and trigger subjects and writing goals will help you communicate with potential critique partners to ensure a good fit.
- Stretch your boundaries to befriend someone. Be cautiously brave as you reach out to potential CPs.
- Use the tools we've provided to get to know potential CPs.
- Attempt a critique practice run. Limit the length of a piece and see if you and your potential CP mesh in more than just knowledge and personality.

QWERTY CHAT

Preparing for a Critique

CHAT FOUR: Preparing for a Critique

COMMUNICATION CENTERS A PARTNERSHIP. We provide you with some specific definitions in this chat, along with some questions to ask and answer with your partner before you exchange critique expectations.

SECTION 1: READY YOUR WORK

When Is Your Work Ready For a Critique?

MEA: Before you submit a piece for critique, you should first prepare your manuscript. We strongly recommend revision time between typing *The End* on the first draft and releasing it to your CP.

JOY: The primary purpose for this is to give you time to bond with your piece. You need to read through your manuscript without outside influence to make sure you understand your theme as best as possible and know the motivations and purposes that drive your work.

QWERTY DEFINITIONS

THEME encompasses the central topic on which a manuscript focuses. It's the glue that holds all the pieces and parts of the writing together, giving the project purpose. Theme affects the author's words and mood choices, character development, plot development—pretty much all aspects of the story. Depending on the author's purpose and genre, theme can be exemplified through character experiences or presented in a thesis statement. Theme may be an exploration of a broad idea like *sacrifice* or of something specific, like *repressing emotions doesn't heal them*.

The **MOTIVATION** behind a piece is the author's driving reason for writing it in the first place. This might be where the author's worldview most comes into play.

The **PURPOSE** of a piece is what the author wants his audience to take away from his writing.

An author's primary reason to understand his motivation and purpose is so he will know when a critique is accurate or when it is an assault on his voice. While this self-awareness must be coupled with all of the knowledge of genre and story structure we reviewed in Chat Two, an author's motivation and purpose in a piece give him the code for understanding his voice. We'll go in more depth on the subject of Author Voice in the next section.

MEA: If you can articulate the theme, motivation and purpose before you hand your piece over, you will receive a more informed critique on other aspects of your story because your partner won't have to figure these things out. Of course, if the theme eludes you, you'll be entering a theme integration critique together, which we'll cover in a moment.

As you finish projects through the years, you may be able to evolve your writing process to include a clear connection to theme, motivation and purpose before you type your first paragraph. However, beginning writers tend to see these foundational elements change between the first page of a draft and the last.

Once you have these nailed down, make the necessary changes you can see with the knowledge of what's most important to you and your purpose in this piece.

JOY: Out of respect for your partner's time and investment, you should clean up what you know needs adjusting before you press *send*. For example, if you've written a memoir that comes in at a whopping 250,000 words, you should know that no memoir should ever be that long. You've got a ton of cutting to do, Friend. Remove what you can and save your CP the unnecessary reading and mental workout.

MEA: Consider swimming pools. The ones you want to jump into without hesitation are those in which you can see the bottom. If your story pool is clear, your readers will want to immerse themselves in it but will be less likely to jump in if the water is cloudy or pesky debris is floating in their way. Your first revision is the same as skimming the leaves off the surface of the pool and inserting the right mixture of chemicals to clear the field of view. Your critique partner will point out the next urgent extractions; then, it's your turn to scoop those chunks out as you revise based upon his suggestions. The ideal end goal is crystal-clear water—the kind that makes you want to yell, "Cannonball!"

JOY: On the other side, some writers are like me and lean more toward the clingy side of things—incessantly tweaking and changing and adapting and never turning it over to someone else. Don't do that either.

After your initial read-through and first revision, let it loose. We promise this will not be the last opportunity for you to get your hands on those words. You could pour in chemical after chemical to your pool and make it far worse instead of better. No one wants a chlorine burn, especially when someone else could come in with a special testing kit and determine exactly what you need to make your water dip-worthy.

MEA: We thought of only two ways we would agree you could skip this initial self-revision. The first would be if you are one of the evolved writers who can articulate these elements to your CP without it. This opinion should be formed by experience and not ego, of course.

The second would be if you and your partner's critique process has altered as you spend more and more time with each other's words. We would expect this to be a decision made after extensive previous work with one another. If it's mutually agreed upon that your piece is sent the moment after you save the first draft or in increments as you complete them, then you have our blessing.

Go forth and critique.

JOY: Other than those exceptions, if you have a critique partner already and have written a piece of fiction or nonfiction that has been through at least one self-revision, it's almost time to activate your CP superpower.

IDENTIFY YOUR THEME, motivations and purpose in one of your works. How can you better implement each? Next, make all the changes you can. Your partner will be glad you did.

SECTION II: TYPES OF CRITIQUES

MEA: We're nearing the hands-on task of critiquing, but we have a few more vital details to discuss before we stain our fingers red. If you and your partner have the same expectations going into this process, you will avoid multiple headaches and get exactly what you need the first time without requesting a redo.

Ask. Us. How. We. Know.

JOY: Definitions for critiques vary from expert to expert, so we thought we'd give you our QWERTY definitions for some common types of critiques. If you and your partner start from the same understanding of the task at hand, your critique experience should flow smoothly.

We're listing a significant number of critique options, but this is a brief and simple overview of these types alone. More critique types exist. Also, understand that you and your critique partner will not use all of these types on every project. You will pick and choose which one(s) you would like your CP to use based on your needs and his strengths.

Do you see now why we spent so much time urging you to list your strengths and weaknesses? You're welcome.

Overall Content Evaluation

QWERTY DEFINITION

An **OVERALL CONTENT EVALUATION CRITIQUE** is what we like to call "the whole shebang." This critique reviews the entire project—theme clarity, story structure, dialogue, character depth and development, plot development and logical consistency, author voice and narrative tone, point of view and pacing, to name a few.

MEA: Two things to expect with an overall content evaluation: First, your partner will point out a little about a lot. The results you receive will be many and varied. Don't let all the notes discourage you. Second, you're asking your partner to consider a ton of issues in one pass. You can expect he will miss things. Also, this is not a short cut to a final product. You will need to absorb the over-arching concepts your partner points out and evaluate your piece again, applying his reactions to specific sections throughout.

Remember, the beauty of working with a CP is you remain in the driver's seat. To maintain that control, you've got multiple rounds of revision work ahead of you. Embrace the process and be thankful for your CP's assistance.

If you're giving this type of critique, remember you're dealing with "big picture" concepts. Don't confuse this with a copy edit and get into grammar and syntax. You'll have enough to do already. Additional comments on aspects you have not agreed on could overwhelm the author. We'll discuss this concept in more detail at the end of this chat.

Theme Integration

QWERTY DEFINITION

A **THEME INTEGRATION CRITIQUE** dissects how the theme is represented in each chapter or scene and across the entire work.

JOY: This is a fun one. Every story has a theme—or should anyway—and, as our definition earlier in this chat reveals, this aspect of a work keeps it all together. The partner providing this critique will focus on how well the chosen theme is woven throughout each chapter, scene or entire work.

MEA: An author can say the theme before the critique, or he can see what the story or article reveals as the partner evaluates the piece. It just depends on you and on your partner's preference.

The origination of theme can come during any creative stage. My story idea bloomed from my theme. The theme was based on personal experience, and I wanted to tell the story to express that specific theme through fiction. Knowing the theme from the beginning, though it may have veered a little, helped me keep the story on track. As I wrote, an unexpected sub-theme became prominent. My story deepened, and the sub-theme lifted my primary theme fully into the spotlight.

When Joy critiqued this story, she called me out on one section where I revealed too much theme-related information too soon. It wasn't organic.

Excerpt from Joy's critique: *I'm wondering if this is too early for such a wide-open-baring-the-soul truth. You and I know Jade, but most readers are still trying to see her. And, BOOM! Girl got major needs-to-be-needed, people-pleaser issues. May need a little more character cushion before this.*

Be careful to allow your theme to develop over time rather than throwing all your playing cards on the table and asking your dealer, "Is this anything good?"

JOY: The solidification of my theme came after a few drafts of *Any Good Thing*. Thanks to my CPs, I finally isolated my primary theme: *mistaking selfishness for sacrifice*. Once that became clear, I could better polish certain scenes to point in that direction.

Whether an author knows his theme before, during or after writing or revisions, this evaluation requires a CP to ask many questions for the author's consideration, especially when the theme is unclear. These questions and a CP's advice will also help the author decide if the theme he chose is right for the story he is telling.

MEA: Like Joy's situation, an author may choose one theme, but, as the piece is written, the focus shifts. A CP may alert the author to a different, more appropriate theme or guide him back to his original one, as circumstances require. The careful CP will also point out any time the author overdoes his theme integration.

Authors are known for using metaphor for theme expression, too. If you read a repetitive metaphor, the CP needs to make sure it is meant to represent the theme or something else equally important. If the metaphor doesn't have a deeper meaning, the repetition isn't necessary. If the metaphor is legitimate, is a clear connection between the theme and the metaphor visible? Does the link to the theme feel natural or forced? The CP should examine if that comparison makes sense every time it shows up.

Dialogue Review

QWERTY DEFINITION

A **DIALOGUE REVIEW CRITIQUE** focuses on consistency in the characters' voices, with particular attention given to the dialogue's purpose, place and conciseness, as well as its natural presentation and flow.

Dialogue and *review* both have straightforward denotations and connotations. So, this one's self-explanatory, right? Not exactly. Dialogue is hard, Partner; and you have a big task ahead of you. Ask five authors how to write dialogue; you'll get ten different answers, each beginning with, "You have to …."

We're not going to say you *have* to do anything because we feel that is a decision best left to each writer. We will offer a few guidelines for evaluating dialogue, though.

Skip To The Meat.

JOY: Readers skip greetings; plus this dialogue "fat," as we'll call it, forms one more layer veiling the purpose of the conversation. If a greeting doesn't include an unexpected revelation about a character or the story, you likely don't need it. Clearing away the chitchat gives dialogue more meaning.

Make Your Greetings Mean Something.

MEA: However, a greeting can sometimes reveal needed character information—like unspoken animosity between characters exemplified in clipped or rude salutations or a hidden affair in an awkward exchange in front of spouses. A CP can evaluate if a greeting should survive the red pen or not.

Pair Dialogue With Action.

JOY: Dialogue pairs well with meaningful action that highlights the sincerity of exchanged words or alludes to an alternate, underlying emotion or meaning in the interaction.

If you have two characters sitting in a room engaged in conversation, this suggestion still applies. Show readers how the characters feel by the way they sit—slumped, straight-backed, relaxed, tensed; by their hands—wringing, white-knuckled, playing with hair or clothing. Does his voice crack? Is he too still, sending chills dancing up and down the other character's spine?

Whatever the action—small or large—it must be there, or your reader won't be able to understand the scene's purpose. Also, it's just a weird mental picture if all you can envision from a dialogue's description are talking heads.

Practice The Art of Subtext.

When appropriate to a scene's purpose, utilize subtext.

QWERTY DEFINITION

SUBTEXT is dialogue that both means what it means and means something deeper.

MEA: It makes your reader the one who decides which meaning the character is expressing at that moment, which can provide a surprise or foreshadowing. It also gifts discoveries to someone who is into a second read. For example, a well-placed "I love you" can be both a declaration of overwhelming emotion and last words of a character preparing to make the ultimate sacrifice.

Keep It Short.

JOY: Dialogue should be concise. Here's an acronym to remember: KISS can stand for "Keep It Short and Simple" or "Keep It Short, Stupid." Choose which one motivates you.

Long pages of dialogue push readers out of the scene, which is the fastest way to lose them. You don't want to do that. The scene is their home. It should be cozy there.

MEA: Sometimes, long informative conversations tell the reader information that should be shown instead. Make your character work for knowledge. If he's just sitting in a room listening to a person drone on about the history of a secret organization and how he holds the missing piece to answer a centuries-long mystery, both character and reader will be bored — secret organization and mystery notwithstanding.

However, if the conversation occurs during a sword fight in an ancient cathedral, you could be on to something. Such a scene would require you to break the conversation into slices of information between parries. Allow your character to find important pieces of information here and there, and then the big backstory reveal will be shorter and more palatable because you've been working up to it, while maintaining pleasant pacing, which we'll discuss more soon.

JOY: Plus, who doesn't love a good sword fight?

Toss The Fillers.

Another way to improve dialogue requires removing fillers. We might slide *ums* and *ahs* into conversational gaps to cover our need for another second of thinking, but we don't want to read them. Characters don't need them, anyway; the author's doing all the thinking, right? In theory, anyway.

Fillers might push readers out of the story. At the very least, readers will skim over them, so it's better to leave them out of the text until you can break the rule well.

Ditch Unnecessary Responses.

MEA: In real life, when we're in conversation and want the person speaking to know we're still invested, we might repeat words like *Sure* or *Yeah* or *Okay*. These aren't necessary in writing if your character is actually invested in the conversation. However, if your character is only pretending to listen, a couple of these responses could then alert the reader to the character's false attentiveness.

Notice any words or phrases your eyes hop over as you read and ask why they didn't hold your attention. Once you've answered that question a few dozen times, you will have a better grasp on good dialogue, and it will change the way you write spoken scenes.

Character Development Analysis

A **CHARACTER DEVELOPMENT ANALYSIS AND CRITIQUE** examines the consistency of a character's speech, interactions, actions and reactions as well as the strength of his internal change over the course of his story. This critique can focus on the protagonist, antagonist or all named or vital characters.

JOY: The reader's relationship to the characters is what will keep him reading until 4:00 a.m. just to find out how it ends. You can see the importance in getting useful feedback on characters' developmental arcs. The first character development analysis you do may need to focus on only one character. As you get more practiced, you could chart multiple at a time.

A few character aspects to analyze include: speech and sentence structure consistency, consistent character behavior and personality and internal problem.

SPEECH CONSISTENCY

Does the character's voice remain consistent in the dialogue?
Does he have the same cadence and mannerisms or tendencies throughout the book?

SENTENCE STRUCTURE CONSISTENCY

MEA: If the character you're evaluating is the narrator, does the prose "sound" like him? Does the character speak in short, blunt sentences; long, descriptive sentences; or poetic, observant remarks? Whatever his style, is it consistent throughout the story? Unless the character has multiple personalities, you should be able to tell. If the character does have multiple personalities, each one should have a consistent sentence structure and speech trait, so I don't really see an exception to this.

Character Behavior

JOY: It's common for characters to have a tell whenever they experience heightened emotions. Some brush hair from their foreheads when frustrated; some bite their thumbnails when they're focused on solving a problem; some wring their wrists or twist jewelry when they're lying or stressed. Whatever it is, you want to make sure a character's physical tell is consistent and linked to corresponding internal struggles.

This is how an author can show the character's internal landscape without telling, so make sure the groundwork is laid. The reader should know exactly what it means when the character tucks her hair behind her ear later in the book when the action is separated from the first description. On the flip side, if this action is overused and becomes annoying, you should alert the author. Readers demand a healthy balance.

Consistent Character Personality

MEA: It is important to pay attention to the logic behind a character's reaction to any situation or decision in any dilemma. For example, if the character was attacked by a giant dragonfly in his fragile pre-teen years, it makes sense that he would run screaming from a dragonfly-infested creek bed as an adult. However, if he's standing there in curious wonder, taking in the kaleidoscope of colors on dragonfly wings fluttering around him, that contradicts his earlier trauma. Readers will lose investment because his response doesn't fall in line with his backstory, unless you walk them through the change.

INTERNAL PROBLEM

JOY: Throughout the story, a character's internal problem should be tested and forged until a newly minted internal makeup is established at the end, for better or worse. Track the journey on paper and make sure the steps to get him from the beginning to the end are logical and justify the new being the character becomes. Change—good or bad—must occur. An end without emotional movement leads to disgruntled readers, not super fans.

Plot Development

QWERTY
DEFINITION

A **PLOT DEVELOPMENT CRITIQUE** weighs the worth of each event—large or small, mostly external but potentially internal, too—against its ability to move the story forward. This critique also uncovers inconsistencies or "holes" in the story.

MEA: Sometimes the author is too close to the story to see that a slight action could unravel his plot, but that's why he has you, right? When asked to provide a plot development critique, you get to read with the purpose of pulling apart your friend's plot. You look for simple solutions to issues or conflicts in order to push the author to strengthen them, so the reader isn't left thinking, *Why didn't the protagonist just call his mom and ask her to push the red button to release the hidden automaton army? I mean, I know the protagonist was an hour away when the aliens attacked, but mom was on the couch reading a book. Is it worth keeping the secret that you're part robot if your entire hometown dies because of it?*

You could be the one to suggest the author should send mom to a much-needed spa weekend retreat for her birthday and—Bam!—nobody is home to push the secret red button. Some conflicts are harder to solve, but you can help the author ask hard questions about his world and story to create ironclad plot scenarios.

JOY: A side benefit to this process is the creation of effective tools to progress your own characters' internal changes. Grab a notepad and pencil to record every scene's plot and the questions you have as you're reading the piece. When you know the whole story, look at your list and decide if it all makes sense.

Are the stakes for the main character high enough in each scene? Are some of the scene's plot points irrelevant to moving the story forward? Is any aspect of the story requiring more willing suspension of disbelief than you're okay with giving? If so, analyze why.

Mull over these questions and share your answers with your partner. Then use the same process for your personal revisions.

Author Voice And Narrative Tone Critique

An **AUTHOR VOICE AND NARRATIVE TONE CRITIQUE** analyzes each technique respectively and determines consistency in each.

AUTHOR VOICE contains the natural sentence structure and word choices unique to an author when he writes. These preferences typically follow the writer across his works.

NARRATIVE TONE is revealed in the consistent emotions the author evokes, generally when he writes in third person omniscient or distant third person. These points of view especially highlight the author's voice.

> Narrative tone is a concoction of the author's word choice, syntax and story.

MEA: First, we must establish that author voice and narrative tone are distinct from one another. In a broader sense, an author's voice should remain consistent across books and even genres. Each writer has distinct ways of communicating from one piece to the next. This is how a writer formulates his stories.

Recognizing your partner's voice is vital to avoid inserting your own voice over his. Is his style verbose? You need to know and accept that; otherwise, you'll be cutting every sentence in half and wondering why he's angry with you. Does he write in a more clipped matter-of-fact manner without much flowery description? If so, suggesting more adjectives could ruin his author voice. Ask yourself if the sentences provide a cadence similar to the author's previous writings.

The author voice is particularly important if your partner is telling his story in distant third person or third person omniscient because he will be the narrator. Therefore, his voice will be a character in the story. Remember, you're looking for consistency—not changing his voice to yours.

When you and your partner set out to learn your author voices, review multiple pieces you've written. Swap and review each other's pieces after you've examined your own. Work together to discover your natural ways of expression or voice. Studying already written pieces keeps you from conscious writing that forces an author voice instead of uncovering your natural one. Through this exercise, you'll learn your voice and your partner's. Plus, you will have accomplished an important task by working together.

JOY: Is the overall narrative tone of the book consistent from beginning to end? In other words, does the book have a distinct emotional feel from the beginning to the end, even through the protagonist's highs, lows and changes? The overall narrative tone should support the author voice and emphasize it on a smaller scale.

An author's chosen vocabulary, syntax and flow in a given scene set the stage for evoking his desired emotion in the reader—remember his purpose we discussed at the start of this chat? On a more specific level, his tone for a scene where two lovers finally confess their undying affection will be vastly different from when a character is about to open a door on a gun barrel.

Your job for this critique is to observe your feelings while reading and explore any time you're emotionally confused or alter your opinion about a person or place within the story. Note these places and share them with the author.

Point of View Consistency

QWERTY
DEFINITION

A **POINT OF VIEW (POV) CONSISTENCY CRITIQUE** checks that the story is told from the same perspective throughout or is consistently and smoothly divided among various points of view.

MEA: One of the most important decisions an author makes is who tells the story and how. He will have one or a set number of narrators generally written in first person or third person. Second person occurs rarely and usually in nonfiction when it does. In this critique, the evaluator will look for consistency in point of view. He will also consider if the author's choice best relays the story. This type of critique combines well with dialogue review and author voice and narrative tone expectations for partners able and willing to take on a few types in one go.

Pacing Review

QWERTY DEFINITION

A **PACING REVIEW CRITIQUE** measures the speed of every scene and determines if it's too fast, too slow or perfect to fit that scene's needs.

JOY: Pacing—in its simplest terms—is the miles per hour of a scene, chapter or book as determined by the author's choice of sentence structure and content. The best way to learn how to analyze pacing is to read widely and observantly.

Notice when you start flipping pages to see when the next chapter starts. Make note of when something happens too quickly and you're confused enough to re-read that section. What you and your partner want is that moment when you're perfectly lost in the story, unaware of speed, space or time. You're living and breathing the story unfolding around you.

Break down when you find the fast, slow and just right scenes and articulate what you think the author did right or wrong. This process will also help you better the pacing in your work as you isolate how to get it right.

MEA: Let's examine a few pacing examples connected to scene types to prepare you for this type of critique.

Writers typically keep action, violence and chase scenes free of unnecessary description and use short, simple sentences with fewer overall words to impart urgency to the reader. They tend to use only the descriptors necessary to show the reader what's happening in the moment—nothing more. A common error in these scenes is making them too short, creating a stunted mental image of the conflict. Make sure your mind's eye sees the scene in full so missing edges won't distract future readers.

JOY: Retrospective scenes describe—in clarity and detail—particular details the character might have missed in the past. They may include sentimental or nostalgic descriptions and lead to flashbacks or childhood recollections. These scenes often run long and can feel slow.

Removing descriptions not linked to the crux of the matter can speed up the pacing. Also, if the protagonist of the scene is involved in a current action—even a simple one, like walking down the street or driving a car—portraying physical interruptions of deeper thinking will guide the reader to feel ongoing forward movement.

We have a perfect example of this in Mea's critique of *Any Good Thing*. I implemented it almost completely because it was such great advice.

Excerpt from Mea's critique: *There needs to be an action or something that ties us to the present story to walk us through this long thought process. Otherwise, Jack's just been standing still for a whole page. Suggestion: Maybe Jack's already running. You can break up this thought by reminding your readers what Jack's doing by the sound of his running cadence on the track, how the emotion of the thought is affecting his running performance, how he rubbed his neck and the memory of the choking tie at Easter. We might need to know information (do we really?), but we don't need to get lost in the past and wandering thoughts.*

MEA: Informative scenes full of vital explanation run the risk of becoming literary bogs. If the information is dispersed in a room with everyone sitting in a circle, place it after an intense action scene, so your reader is ready for an emotional time-out and gets the answers needed as well. You could combine action with information, like we suggested earlier with secrets tossed out between sword thrusts.

Combining or staggering scenes based on the type of emotions they conjure in the reader adds interest and novelty to necessary but traditionally slow scenes and tightens up the overall pacing.

Covering all critique types, though, are the CP's guiding, thoughtful questions of purpose and need for each detail—from characters to information to entire scenes. Without a clear role in moving along the flow of a story, some of these aspects may need to go.

Nonfiction Critique

A **NONFICTION CRITIQUE** often requires a more overall approach and necessitates that the evaluator considers the piece's purpose, topic relevance, structure and logical progress, primary question (and its resulting answer or answers) and clarity in the author's point of view.

JOY: Let's examine a few considerations for critiquing nonfiction pieces such as biographies, memoirs and academic and essay compilations.

Connecting Thread

The first step in this type of critique is to determine the work's purpose. What is the connecting thread of this piece?

QWERTY DEFINITION

A **CONNECTING THREAD** is the central idea or question that connects the work from beginning to end.

Topic Relevancy

MEA: Before a critique, the author should share with his partner his defense as to why this topic is relevant, necessary and timely. Without this reasoning, the CP could be missing key information to catch areas where the piece could take hold of an opportunity, bringing validation to its topic or eliminating information that doesn't matter.

Readers need to know why they're taking time out of their lives to read a book. Why is its content relevant for their life situation? This is what Joy likes to call the "So what?" point. For example, our primary reason for writing this book is stated in the introduction of this book, clear and simple. "A critique partnership ripe with respect, knowledge, effort and communication can help both you and your partner get where you want to be faster with greater proficiency." Each word we add after that declaration should defend its claim.

Structure Choice

JOY: It's important to know the author's structure choice, which is generally decided upon by the author before the drafting process. For example, before beginning to write this book, we had a discussion on how to organize it to be most useful for its audience and adjusted our plan as our book formed.

We divided each chat into four main sections: a brief explanation of our topic, discussion of that information through two or more sections, at least one practical application for each section to guide readers to action and a bullet-point recap of the entire chat. We critiqued each other's sections with this structure fresh in our minds.

Primary Question And Clarity In Answers

MEA: The author needs to reveal the primary question his work answers, especially for informative nonfiction. The critique partner is tasked with making sure the body of the work answers the question as well as supports or defends its answer (or answers). Without the initial question, the CP's job becomes laborious.

Here are a few examples:

Can a person overcome their past and thrive after a horrific childhood accident?
Answer: Yes, and this memoir is proof.
How does reading to children from birth benefit them?
Answer: Greatly, and this article is proof.
How can a writer cultivate and nurture a healthy critique partner relationship?
Answer: By being considerate and intentional with requests, consistent and honest with critiques and knowledgeable yet teachable with a willingness to improve together—and this book is proof. (See what we did there?)

JOY: If you know the primary question going into a critique, it will be easier to see if the body of the work holds a satisfying answer. The answer, however, should be withheld. If the partner critiquing has the central question in his mind as he evaluates the piece and answers it incorrectly, the author will know something didn't translate. That would be a great place to begin revisions.

MEA: What do you need to help your partner with this critique? Logical reasoning and a notepad. As you read each section of the piece, create a shorthand outline. If any parts don't clearly and logically answer the original question, then you're prepared with the proof of your notes to show the author. He can analyze your outline to see if any points are not what he meant to emphasize. He can also rework problem sections using that outline as a guide. Sometimes an author is so familiar with the topic, he chalks some details up to basic knowledge, too simple to require coveted word space. If the person critiquing doesn't understand the author's message, though, it's likely future readers will also be lost.

Consistency In Tone

Take note, too, that the piece's tone is consistent throughout. This is frequently done through point of view and word choice. For example, we primarily stick with a second person informal over third person formal so this book feels like a conversation between friends. We wanted to create the mood of a cozy writing workshop retreat or our weekly podcast. We hope you feel we achieved that!

Clear Identification Of The Author's Position On The Topic

JOY: In persuasive nonfiction pieces, the author may present opposition to his stance and negation to that opposition. However, if the piece doesn't clearly identify the author's position on the topic, the argument loses traction. Creating an outline of oppositional fronts and the author's negation to those fronts will help identify if his stance shines and if he retains the final word.

For informational pieces, the goal may be an unbiased, neutral author stance. If so, make sure the descriptors and verbs present connotations that complement the work's needs.

OUR CHALLENGE FOR YOU this section is to review the types of critiques and jot down anything you aren't sure you understand. Take further time to research and study those topics.

Better yet, complete this challenge with your critique partner. He may answer some of your questions, and you might fill in the gaps for him. At the very least, you can split up the study and come back together to report what you each learn. The idea is to come together with the same definitions and understanding of each critique type, so you're prepared to practice them effectively.

Section III: Expectations For Critique Presentation

Timelines and Deadlines

MEA: All writers with a publication goal should have deadlines for each stage of their projects, or they may never let go of their pieces to make something new. This is doubly true when working with others who have the same goal because each person has time expectations and must work critique needs around each other's schedules. If you don't meet your deadline, you've also affected your partner's schedule. Editors, publishing companies, cover artists, agents and other professionals require deadlines, so it's good practice that you and your partner outline individual and joint timelines.

Set a deadline for your first critique that you both believe is attainable and forgive your partner if he needs more time. Likewise, don't assume your partner didn't give it his all if he returns his results early. Once you've completed your first round of critiques, you'll be able to compare the time you thought it would take with actual time. It's this constant evaluating of your process that will eventually lead you to a predictable routine.

We add a week for unexpected situations. This is an absolute must if you have children or aging parents or someone else who relies on you. Illnesses, unexpected emergencies and accidents can happen to everyone. Consider that week your time insurance.

JOY: If you're up against an incredibly tight deadline, make that clear from the beginning. For example, you can't expect your partner to be able to turn around a full manuscript critique in a week ... beginning tomorrow.

This is where multiple critique partners may be advantageous. With multiple partners, odds should improve to receive at least one critique when an opportunity pops up. This is where communication is, once again, crucial. Written communication for details like this is often the best policy.

Throw in a little extra politeness when asking for a quick turnaround on a critique. Here's an example: "I know it's short notice, but I saw this contest today. I'd love to enter my article on boll weevils as polished as possible. Are you willing and able to provide an overall critique by November 12? Thanks for thinking on it!"

MEA: Even with planning ahead, a time buffer and strong communication, life happens. When it does, priorities shift and unavoidable delays occur. If you are in the process of critiquing and something derails your progress past that built-in week, inform the author immediately. Explain the situation. Be realistic and apologetic. Be certain the delay is unavoidable, and then do everything in your power to present an achievable second deadline and meet it.

If your partner is the one with the delay, extend grace and understanding. Consider if the second timeline could work. If not, ask for the critique back as it is and utilize it as best you can. Some critique is better than no critique, and you may see suggestions that apply throughout your piece.

The "Unlucky" CP

JOY: Okay, let's be real for a minute. As we've already said, life does happen; however, for some, life seems to "happen" every week. Either a partner like this is incredibly unlucky or he hasn't figured out how to time manage or properly determine how long a task takes him. If this becomes a regular occurrence, his partner should reevaluate the relationship to determine if the constant disregard for timelines is worth working through and talking over. If not, that partner may consider cutting ties.

Compensation Clarity

MEA: Set and define all boundaries of your critiquing relationship, including expected compensation. Typically, this works out in the nature of a give-and-take relationship. You critique a piece; he critiques a piece. If, however, one of you hits a busy patch where you no longer have the time to critique, be transparent with this change in availability and work out another form of compensation. Better yet, review your responsibilities to see if you can fulfill the requests you and your partner stated at the beginning. The word *partner* denotes an equivalency, but it's best to readdress that so you each understand that whatever you ask of one another, you are obligated to reciprocate.

Above & Beyond: When Critique Partners Do More Than What's Expected

JOY: Some writers have more tools in their critiquing boxes than others. If this describes your critique partner, rejoice! He has more knowledge to share. Perhaps he has editing experience and gives you more detailed feedback for line edits. Maybe he is familiar with trademarks and can tell you when you need to change something specific to something more generic. He may even offer real-time comments inside your document as he reads, so you're getting an in-the-moment glimpse at reader reactions to your story. These are all more than a base-level critique, and your CP is giving you a gift.

That gift may feel more like a punishment at first glance, though. If full line edits coupled with a critique send you spiraling, tell your partner. Show gratitude, communicate and adjust.

If you have multiple partners, maybe you have some give you straightforward critiques, make those revisions and then have your grammar whiz friend give you an editing onceover. Clarify what he can give you without tainting the message with negativity. Be sure you're both on the same page with the expected basics for a critique and then discuss extras separately.

MEA: Sometimes you don't know what part of a critique will overwhelm you until you receive your partner's hard work. I didn't know what my reaction would be until Joy returned my first novel critique. It bled red, and a conglomeration of first-response emotions, line edits and overall developmental notes threatened to do me in. I felt all the emotions: dejection, doubt, anger, disbelief, embarrassment, unworthiness. I then fixated on the fact that I hadn't the knowledge to make those corrections myself without someone's help. That was pride, folks; and there's little room for excessive pride when you create.

I walked outside, breathed in the God-given air and reflected on my relationship with Joy. No past action led me to believe Joy was trying to purposely hurt me. Joy cared for me and my success in this crazy dream. This didn't come from a malicious attack or revenge tactic or an unhealthy confidence boost; that just wasn't Joy. I decided everything red was an opportunity to make my book its best.

Once I returned to the critique, I found some of the comments were compliments ... written in red. Others were responses to areas outside of my expertise, but most aided plot and character development. I had expected only those last details but received so much more—and have present-day appreciation for them. At the time, I didn't know I had a red-type trigger to tell Joy about. She knows now. It's that whole communication thing again.

I hope you'll be kind, have a private freak-out response moment, think through the situation and then get to work. Once you're separated from the moment, update your critique partner about your new knowledge, like I did. Try not to be embarrassed. We learn things about ourselves all the time. Life is a perpetual practice to become better. Receiving critiques has helped me internalize the fact that I am not perfect, and the only way to fail is to settle in and ignore the push to be better.

JOY: If your partner goes above and beyond on some critiques but cannot on others, don't throw a fit or resent him for sticking to the basics. Anything your partner can supply betters your piece. He's not trying to sabotage your work. He's just saying he can't, for example, mark every sentence for passive voice or mention more than three prepositional phrases this critique like he did last time. Discuss that and respect his time.

Each new manuscript requires a fresh discussion on expectations and type of presentation specific to that project. Our Critique Structure Questionnaire in Appendix D can help.

If your partner can't provide another extravagant critique this time, consider the first a treat and remember that, thanks to that initial experience, you now know many of your natural tendencies and should be working toward improving them. During self-revisions, fix the common issues your partner revealed. Making these changes before you hand your next piece over shows your appreciation and his effectiveness.

MEA: Due to the amount of time it takes to give a thorough critique on long works, reviewing a manuscript more than once may not be something your partner can do. However, he may. It never hurts to ask.

If you want to read your friend's manuscript again after he revises it, let him know you're willing to do that for him. If you have the time, it can be satisfying because you're seeing firsthand how the author took your suggestions, questions and feedback and used them to improve the manuscript. This is where the choice to start with a short story helps again. Because of their length, short stories are easier to give a second hit than a full book manuscript, while still teaching just as much about each other's styles, preferences and abilities.

A quick brainstorming session through a chat or email can guide you to a breakthrough when you're stuck on something during revisions and your partner has read the entire piece.

Not all critiquing deals directly with the work in progress. Think ahead to descriptions and query letters, book proposals and pitches, if these apply to your overall goals. Do you need help with those? On the other side, would you have time to give this type of feedback when the time comes? Assuming your partner will help with those could strain your partner's time resources and good graces. Asking proves you respect him and acknowledges you believe his responsibilities are important. Even when you're quite sure your partner would say "Yes," ask anyway.

A *no* is not a personal attack. Your partner is being honest and probably feels badly about having to pass. Put away your snark for a more appropriate time and tell your partner you understand—because you do, right? Time is finite. You will have to turn your partner down from time to time, too. Forcing guilt on your partner to do what you want may get you immediate gratification but will chip away the good parts of your partnership.

If you know your CP is working on something connected to the work you critiqued, offer to help if you have the time. Your partner may not have considered you would be available to help beyond the manuscript or he may not want to ask too much of you. But, you're a fan of the piece now. You've helped it go from good to great. You've fallen for the ticking parts of the piece's heart. Maybe now you want to support how the story gets shared with the world. If so, support your partner by offering your help.

QWERTY CHALLENGE

MAKE A CHART OF what you think are standard CP responsibilities and which are "above and beyond" the call of critique partner duty. Have your expectations changed since the beginning of this book? As you're thinking about the needs of your work in progress, make sure you're not exhausting your CP with above-and-beyond requests.

It's time to write out the information you need to give or have before embarking on a critique. We know what you're thinking.

QWERTYs, didn't you already discuss all of this stuff in the last section?

Well, yes ... and no.

The information in the previous section referred to a global view of you, your goals and needs. This round of questions is specific to the piece you're now asking your partner to review. You know each other now; you've talked about how you need your critiques to be presented. Now it's time to get down to the specifics of this project. You'll find a Critique Structure Questionnaire in Appendix D. If you have answers to both the overall view of your critique needs and the specific details of each critique, you will receive the most beneficial feedback and avoid many frustrating misunderstandings.

Recap

- Your work is ready for critique once you have a completed piece you've bonded with and self-revised.
- Partners with the same definitions and ideas regarding types of critique evaluations simplify communication regarding project needs.
- Shared project goals and expectations are powerful, time-saving tools. Be sure to discuss these in detail.
- Notice when your partner goes above and beyond and when he may need more help than he's asking for. Also, guard against either of you making unreasonable requests.

QWERTY CHAT

Giving a Critique

CHAT FIVE:
Giving a Critique

WE HAD NO IDEA how to give a critique when we got started, so this chat breaks down lessons we've learned through our experiences, in hopes you don't have to spend time finding these nuggets on your own.

Section I: Communication

Clear Communication Requires Extra Care.

JOY: Every success or failure we've had as critique partners has stemmed from solid communication or a lack thereof. That's why we believe clear and simple communication is the key to the strongest partnerships.

We recognize that regardless of your method of communication—email, messaging, video chat, phone call or face-to-face—something will be miscommunicated.

That's the nature of conversation, unfortunately. We admit the convenience of technology is only in relation to location. Using digital forms of communication requires us to work harder to give and receive clear messages.

The best chance for your words to relay clearly will come through a face-to-face conversation coupled with written expectations, like you'll get by using our handy-dandy Critique Structure Questionnaire in Appendix D.

MEA: Joy and I believe a common communication fault is not focusing solely on the conversation. In other words, you're not truly listening to one another—or reading for comprehension. In a natural world of busying oneself to oblivion and a digital world that never sleeps, we struggle to focus on the words someone says and the subtext behind them. We're here to tell you that you will miss something in communication; but we can give you some tips to potentially avoid that outcome or to bounce back after a misstep.

Repeat Everything Back In Your Own Words.

Sometimes we hear the exact words another person says; but, in our minds, we define those words differently or reorder them in the way we absorb them. When you're in the fast food drive-through and the worker doesn't repeat your order or it flashes too quickly on the screen for you to review, does a sense of dread cool your veins? Me, too! Why? I think it's because almost every time I haven't been able to confirm the worker received the message, I've had to remove onions from my burger.

JOY: If your partner—like the fast food worker—doesn't repeat your expectations (order), ask him to do so. That's a life lesson, Friend. You don't have to passively sit by and wonder if you're going to get the bacon-lettuce-pickle-hold-the-mayo. Just ask, "Would you repeat my order?" or "Can we make sure we're on the same page, please?" This little bit of boldness could help you avoid frustration and a culmination of incidents that eventually mutate into a bitter monster.

Here's an example. Let's say Mea asks me to include a chapter analysis with my critique and I eagerly agree. I read Mea's book and jot down notes about big overall impressions for each chapter. When I'm done, I send Mea a one-page document with my overall impressions and critique of the book as a whole and a sentence or two on some of the chapters that stood out with either positive or negative aspects.

MEA: What I might have expected was a more encompassing evaluation on each chapter. Did it move the character along somehow? Were the scenes well executed and purposeful? Did they transition well within the chapter and between chapters? Did the pacing match each chapter's action? Were there any inconsistencies in a chapter or plot holes or unanswered questions?

In this situation, I'm disappointed with what Joy gave me ...

JOY: And I'm oblivious and happy with my personal performance. I believe I discovered some gems about Mea's book that she can polish, resulting in better characters, theme and overall story execution.

MEA: Those are appreciated; however, I expected notes on things Joy likely noticed but didn't write down because she didn't think she was asked to. Because of poor communication at the onset, this situation could be the foundation of my believing that Joy is a lousy critique partner or isn't as knowledgeable as she claims to be. Our partnership would deteriorate.

To avoid this scenario, I could have asked Joy for her understanding of my request. "Hey! I know I quickly ran through what I need. Would you tell me what you heard to make sure I communicated clearly?"

JOY: Or, I could have stopped for a moment to consider Mea's request and respond with, "Let me make sure I know exactly what you want. Should I include thoughts on a chapter when they stand out along with my overall book reactions? If nothing major sticks out for a chapter, just ignore it?"

MEA: I might reply something like, "I had really hoped you could evaluate each chapter for purpose, pacing, transitions, inconsistencies and plot holes. Would you be able to do that as you go or is that too much to ask?"

JOY: And, I could reply. "Oh! I'm so glad we clarified that! Yes, I would be happy to do that. So, I will give you an overall impression of the book with reflections on your theme, character and plot development. I will also include an analysis on each chapter for its purpose, pacing, flow, inconsistencies and plot holes. Anything I'm missing?"

MEA: This project might have me feeling insecure, so I could find the courage to add, "If you could let me know how I'm doing on transitions between scenes, too, that would be great. I'm a little worried about a few of the earlier chapters, especially. Some spots felt abrupt to me, but I'm not sure."

JOY: With this addition, I'll clarify one more detail. "Gotcha! I will keep an eye out for abrupt or jarring chapter and scene endings and starts. Do you want to tell me the specific spots you're concerned about or would you rather me notice them organically?"

MEA: "See if you notice them, please. That way we'll know it's definitely an issue, and I'm not just pushing my paranoia on you!"

JOY: "Makes perfect sense!"

Now, this back-and-forth conversation we acted out constitutes only step one in necessary repetition. I know my forgetfulness, so I will add a second step—writing down the details. I will pull out pen and paper or note-taking app and take notes as we talk—or use our questionnaire template stored in our shared online folder. This provides an extra layer of clarity to our process. Plus, I can read it back to Mea for a triple repeat.

While I might be more forgetful than you are, I hope you won't skip these steps just to prove your memory is superior to mine. Challenge me to a matching game instead. I can almost guarantee you'll win.

MEA: If you follow these steps and your partner doesn't provide the agreed-upon information, your problem may not be fixed easily. Talk to your partner and try a few more critiques if you like; but, remember, you're not obligated to continue a relationship that is not mutually beneficial.

If you are the one who is not providing the information you've discussed, apologize and make a commitment to listen and serve your partner better. If you do not want to continue the relationship, just say so. Don't waste the other's time by returning bad critiques and stringing him along. Some people work out better as friends; and, if you handle the situation well, you could still have that friend when the partnership is over.

Back to our example, if we didn't have that clarifying conversation and Joy presented me with a critique lacking much of what I expected, it's vital for the continuation and growth of our partnership for me to bring the miscommunication to Joy's attention. I can't sweep the dirt under the rug and pretend it's not there.

I could set up the conversation like this: "Hey Joy! I wanted to thank you for giving your time to read my manuscript. I appreciated your insights on my dialogue tags and the questions you asked about my main character's motivations. They helped me dive deeper and flesh out who the character really is and what her underlying motivations are. I do have a question for you, though, regarding the chapter analysis. When I asked for that, I realize I may not have been clear. I had hoped to get your reactions to my execution of each chapter: purpose, pacing, transitions—between scenes and between chapters—as well as any inconsistencies or plot holes that popped out at you. Would you have time to think through these details for each of the chapters? If not, I understand, especially since you've already evaluated the piece. I just thought maybe it would still be fresh since you finished reading last night."

JOY: I might respond with, "I'm so sorry I didn't clarify exactly what you wanted. I feel so silly, especially since we wrote a book about critique partners and the need for healthy communication. Thank you for telling me! I would be happy to do that. I did notice some details about the pacing, and there was one transition that felt a little rough. Let me check my notes for anything else. Can you give me until next Wednesday to get it back to you? I'm going out of town over the weekend but can jot down some bullet points now and type it up in better detail for you the first part of the week."

MEA: My relief would quickly morph into gratitude. "Sure! Thank you so much! And, next time, I'll make it a point to be clearer."

JOY: Mea has bolstered our partnership by being honest with the failed expectation, which alerted us that we need better clarity in the future. By each of us accepting responsibility for our parts in the confusion, we've solidified the continuation of our partnership.

MEA: We also improved our communication skills for other life relationships. And, by working together to find a solution that works within Joy's timeline while still giving me all I need for a more successful revision, we reiterated the value we place on one another's time and work.

Strive For Clarity Within A Critique.

JOY: Clarity should continue during a critique. When we critique another person's work, it's sometimes hard to verbalize what we think the problem is or how our friend might correct it. In these cases, a metaphor referencing life or an example from our own writing experiences may help clarify our point. You might be tempted to skip over an issue you spot because you're unsure how to word the problem.

Please don't.

MEA: You could be second-guessing if an issue even exists since you can't quite pinpoint it, but trust your instincts. Devote the time to pick apart your thoughts, get to the core of what's bothering you about that section and flesh out how to explain it. If you discover it's not a problem, fine.

What if you do nothing? You'll hinder your partner and yourself. The more you practice turning your reactions into words, the better you become at it; so, as much as your partner will benefit from knowing what you found, you will also benefit from the translation practice. It gets easier; we promise. Don't give up.

Ask Questions To Help The Author Process Your Concerns.

JOY: Sometimes neither the story nor the author provides enough information to suggest a specific fix. How can you help your partner when what you need to structure a resolution is missing? You switch your commentary to questions.

Often, the best critique you can offer is a well-placed question. Questions guide the author to his own conclusions without inserting your assumptions or preferences into his story.

Construct them with genuine curiosity. Let wonder guide you. You should put aside any natural sarcasm or negativity. Neither approach will be effective here and could be destructive to your relationship.

MEA: Questions present opportunities for an author to dive deeper into an aspect of his plot or characters he hadn't previously considered. Through questions, you show him where bones still peek through, where skin is missing or where a joint is needed to make an appendage function. You may not know what joints you have to choose from in order to move the section toward its ultimate goal, but you can point out when one is missing. The author can then hop in and pick the right one to get the job done.

As the author, you need to communicate with clarity in response to the critique. If any comments or questions don't make sense, ask for clarification. Even if you think you've figured out what he's saying, you're never wrong to ask again. You could have mistaken his intention and based a revision around wrong information—which is a thing of nightmares.

JOY: Plus, you never know when questions could result in brainstorming solutions over cookie dough and a giant jar of pickles. And, who doesn't love cookie dough and pickles?

MEA: Do I have to eat both at the same time or is it one food item per partner? Please, clarify. Also, dibs on the cookie dough!

Give More Than Radio Silence.

Before we take a snack break, we have one more note on communication: if you are critiquing a long piece, drop the author a line once or twice during your process. It will boost his confidence and ease his worry over knowing someone else is reading his words. It can be simple and quick: "Chapter 13—when the girl trips over the dragon's tail and lands in the centaur's arms—I actually snorted!"

He gets a quick assurance that you are enjoying his story and an update that you are, indeed, reading and progressing nicely and on track with your timeline.

JOY: While each of the examples we share in this section focused on fiction critiques, all the same advice applies to nonfiction.

Communication is key, regardless of the type of project under critique.

QWERTY CHALLENGE

THINK OVER A RECENT conversation with your partner—or someone else if you haven't found your CP yet. Write out in your own words what you understood. Ask him if you got the message right. How can you improve future communications?

Section II: Tone

Present Critiques In Your Conversational Voice.

MEA: It's easy to put on our professional critiquing hat and role-play as a fancy businessperson. You can do that if it helps you get through the draft; but, when it comes to sharing your findings, don't lose your personality and your personal connection to the writer you're helping. Seeing *you* in the comments will make it easier for him to accept the harder things you have to say.

When you're thinking of examples to convey what you're suggesting, draw them from shared experiences instead of cliché. Choose books you've both read or stories you've created together. It will be more fun for both of you that way, and your friend will know *exactly* what you're trying to say.

Shared memories provide more example possibilities or welcome anecdotes. Does the line where a squirrel sneaks up on a dragon and he shoots fire out of his nose remind you of something? Maybe the time y'all ate at a Mexican restaurant and you shot margarita through your nose when a mariachi band snuck up behind you? It's okay to say so in a comment. If you were face-to-face with your partner, you would say it; so why not remind your partner that you're his friend in between corrections and considerations?

JOY: There's a need for caution, though. You might have an excessively snarky personality and think that tossing sarcastic comments into a critique offers good comic relief. We think that's fantastic; however, if your critique partner struggles with sarcasm in print or your quip doesn't come across in the manner you intend, you've laid the groundwork for a giant misunderstanding.

As you're developing your relationship, rein in anything easily misinterpreted. Once you get to know each other better, you'll be able to include more of your personality in critiques. You'll also be able to "hear" your partner's comments in his voice. Call it a perk of knowing someone so well. You just know when he's joking in a text, email or manuscript critique.

Once you get to this point, fly your sarcastic flag high and fill that critique up. It will be a welcome addition to the mundane at that point, and you can have a good laugh over video chat while you plan your next projects.

Critique The Work, Not The Author.

MEA: Some people want concise, to-the-point feedback, and we respect that. I love a quick, honest phrase to get my writing in line. However, blunt should not equal insulting. You can state a comment simply without flowery niceties but should never add an author attack. You're evaluating his story, not him.

We have heard or experienced critiques (not from each other) that have attacked an author's moral credibility, mental state, parentage or legal right to write or procreate. We have also heard and/or experienced critiques that placed the evaluator on a pedestal, lifting his abilities and opinions above the author's through degrading statements like how his time could have been better used than in reading a manuscript so beneath him.

JOY: Have you received a critique like this? We mourn with you because we know how painful it can be. We hope you find the strength to continue creating and applaud you for the bravery to approach the critiquing table again. A mutually uplifting and building partnership will be a welcome reward for your tenacity to rise above that previous experience.

If you have given a critique like this, even unintentionally or in jest, put down this book and determine why you wrote those comments. It could be you never realized what you did until just now. Or, your reason could run deeper. Make amends where needed.

MEA: If, however, it was intentional, we challenge you to ask yourself some hard questions. What made you want to make someone else hurt? Do you have some insecurities you've been too afraid to admit? Do you have unspeakable pain in your past that you need professional guidance to understand and process?

When you're on the path toward healing, apologize to the author. He deserves to hear it. Whether you are able to speak to the author or not, we hope you can forgive yourself. We forgive you. We've all done things we whole-heartedly regret at some point in our lives. When you're ready, move past it and make better choices from here on out.

Infuse Your Honesty With Tact.

JOY: It's inevitable. You'll have to deliver some harsh truth bombs at one point or another, but it's up to you if they prove fatal or release a puff of momentary, uncomfortable pepper smoke. If you're not careful, you could blow up the foundation of the partnership you've built. Writing, *I cannot believe you think people would actually want to read about dragon robots who turn into ninjas!* is unnecessarily harsh. Frankly, it's plain mean.

Also, it's false. Bring on all the dragon robots who turn into ninjas, I say!

MEA: For the sake of argument, though, if you have a legitimate concern about your friend's story choice, frame it more diplomatically. How about, *Have you considered the audience for a dragon robot ninja book? Do you think it would be large enough to justify working on this book for a year?*

A well-constructed, well-placed question could help your partner reach his own conclusions. Just because the idea isn't your jam, don't diminish your partner's passion for his story. Highlight the positives around the negative, so you're not just harping on what you consider the project missteps.

QWERTY TIP

Re-read your comments and commentary before sending them to your partner. Delete anything that attacks the person rather than the problem. If something lacks tact or compassion, erase and reword it.

JOY: Remember, your suggestions, though educated and requested, arise from your opinions. Statements like, "Fill-in-the-blank might make this section shine." or "Maybe fill-in-the-blank could help with the problem you spoke of." give the author room to consider how he feels about what you think he should do. The occasional "I think …" or "In my opinion …" reminds the author that a critique is your reaction and not law.

Definitive comments that sound more like fact—such as "You need to remove fill-in-the-blank and replace it with more fill-in-the-blank." and "You have to change the main character's repetitive behavior, like, immediately."—lead an author to build defenses toward his partner and any future suggestions, especially if he made that creative choice intentionally. A tactful question regarding a character's behavior allows the author to share his thought process with you. From there you can have an open discussion about the potential issue in his work.

Another option we would recommend requires a special formula.

A well-constructed truth bomb commends the author's creativity or accomplishments, presents your opinion and leaves room for further discussion.

QWERTY Critique Truth Bomb Formula:
Commendation + Opinion + Discussion = Effective Truth

MEA: Let's consider our dragon robot ninjas again. I might say, "I can see the passion you have for this topic in the deep development of your main dragon character." This part of the commentary commends the author's creativity.

"As much as I want the dragon robot Bosch to be my personal ninja, I think the fantastic nature of these creatures reads a little cartoonish, despite your development. My suggestion would be to evaluate the market and the preferences of your potential readership." This part presents your opinion.

"I haven't done a thorough study and could certainly be wrong, but I think it's definitely worth the research to answer these questions before you invest more time." This part leaves room for further discussions. You've spoken your mind; your relationship remains strong; the next move is the author's.

REFLECT ON CRITIQUES GIVEN on your writing. What did you respect about them? What made you frustrated? What aspects, if any, motivated you to continue through to revision? What aspects, if any, made your creative self want to hide in a dark corner for the next decade? Write your answers down and consider the importance of critiques. As you contemplate your responsibility to critique candidly and kindly, determine how presentation might help the author fly or fall.

Recall a moment when you should have delivered a truth bomb. If you don't have a literary example, pick a disagreement in your life. Write down how you would present your thoughts regarding that tough subject using the QWERTY Critique Truth Bomb Formula, which can be tailored to your needs, of course.

See the good and commend the other person + Present your opinion on the controversial topic + Leave room for discussion (genuinely recognize another perspective or, if truthful, your limited knowledge/research).

We're not asking you to present yourself as less than the other person in the "leave room for discussion" variable. You should admit when your knowledge doesn't extend to something as specific as audience size for niche books, though. Your CP is unlikely to be an expert on the audience you writer for either, unless you write in the same genres. Further, by considering another perspective, you may develop compassion or clarity where you once had none.

SECTION III: FOCUS AND PROCESS

Get Specific And Always Give A Reason.

JOY: You shouldn't drop a truth bomb and leave, though. Continuing with our previous example, you've just expressed your concern over the story choice itself and called your partner's dream creatures "cartoonish." The next question most likely directed toward you will be, "How are my dragon robots cartoonish?" So, what do you do?

MEA: You answer it before it's even asked. Why is that our rule, Joy?

JOY: Because you always, always, always back up big assertions with specifics. And, calling your partner's dragon robots "cartoonish" is a giant assertion.

You may not have all the facts related to the hordes of cool readers who want more dragon robot ninjas, but you do have story and character development knowledge; and now's the time to use it. Kindly point out the moments that made you wince and think, "Am I reading a cartoon episode?" and then explain what about those moments seems drawn on. (Get it? It's a pun!)

MEA: These kinds of issues may be hard for the author to see spread over a 400-page manuscript of a story that's vivid as reality in his mind, but you can pull out specific scenes where the actions and dialogue take you back to childhood Saturday morning cartoons. To be proactive, I would add specificity to my previous truth bomb to make my reason more clear.

"I can see the passion you have for this topic in the deep development of your main dragon character.

"As much as I want dragon robot Bosch to be my personal ninja, I think the fantastic nature of these creatures reads a little cartoonish, despite your development. In Chapter Three, your description of his bouncing through the woods reminded me of that bouncy cartoon tiger, especially when he knocked over the grumpy older dragon. Also, in Chapter Five, Bosch's dialogue makes him sound scholarly, whereas he sounds far more childlike in Chapter Six.

"My suggestion would be to evaluate the market and the preferences of your potential readership. I haven't done a thorough study and could certainly be wrong, but I think it's definitely worth the research to answer these questions before you invest more time. If you feel confident with the size of your book's audience, then a little more realism and consistency in the mannerisms, actions and dialogue of your characters will take your story to the next level for those readers."

JOY: This feedback maintains our primary concern—the validity of this book—while showing a commitment to the author's future and highlighting ways to help him improve. So, let's say the author discovers reputable sources that state dragon robot ninjas are the next vampires. Huzzah! The story lives, and we have a plan to polish it for those discerning readers.

MEA: Let's revisit our QWERTY Critique Truth Bomb Formula from earlier and add specificity to the equation.

> **QWERTY Critique Truth Bomb Formula:**
> *Commendation + Opinion + Discussion = Effective Truth x Specificity = Truth Bomb That Slays*

Your next step is to provide further specific feedback to make the dragon robot ninjas more palatable for a reader such as yourself. If the author can win the reluctant reader of dragon robots—over, then the chances are good he'll gather a greater pool of readers overall—those who say things like, "I don't normally read books about dragon robots, but I couldn't put this down!" And, if he's planning on publishing and selling his story, that's exactly what he wants.

JOY: How do you develop a deeper attention to specifics? Practice and persistence. When you reach a part in the story where your instincts are making you think something is terribly wrong, simply commenting, "This just doesn't work for me." is less than helpful. Honestly, it's lazy. Dig deeper to find out why the characters or plot isn't resonating.

While this may be a hard step for you, it will drive you to become a better critique partner, a deeper thinker and a more careful reviewer. And, the next time you write a piece, you will most likely prevent the same mistakes from happening in your own early drafts.

Push past your personal preferences and think back to your interview questionnaire. You told your partner you respect all forms of literature. You didn't exclude science fiction or fantasy. You can find something in the piece to respect, even if it's just a well-told tale; and you know you respect your partner, so release your pre-formed opinions and evaluate how this passage works in light of the writer's story world, goals and purpose.

MEA: You can take off your blinders and try something new. We know you can.

> If you're having trouble connecting with a nonhuman character, remember all main and secondary characters—whether a toaster, robot, bear, flea or flying car—are personified characters with human characteristics. Find the emotional character arc, and you can then begin connecting with the hurting dragon robot, the talking car, the feeling flea.

Don't believe us? Watch *Minuscule: Valley of the Lost Ants* and tell us that broken, persistent, empathetic ladybug doesn't capture your heart and make you invested in his journey. Actually, don't tell us. We don't want to know you're a heartless automaton.

JOY: Automatons are cool. Anyway, back to the "cartoonish" example, once the critique partner knows the author will continue with the story, he should note more specific spots where he felt pulled out of scenes. Then, he should share some potential explanations for the issue.

MEA: He could suggest solutions such as, "I think having a clumsy dragon robot made it feel more playful and 'cartoonish.' Robots, as carefully designed as you explain these to be, could be graceful, could they not? Another potential solution could be to explain the design flaw that makes this particular dragon trip so frequently. The right reason might make him endearing instead of confusing. If you want to video chat next week, we can talk it out then."

JOY: Specifics open your critiquing mind and thought process to your partner, helping him know exactly what you're attempting to communicate. He will then have a solid starting point for revisions. As he's finding solutions for the challenges you mentioned, the author develops a confidence for continuing. Citing specific instances in a critique is further proof the critiquing partner acts from a perspective of knowledge and a belief that the story is fixable—and worthy of the revision process—rather than negatively inserting personal bias.

Give Outside Examples.

Outside examples provide one way to take specificity a step further and explain theories or ideas that can be difficult to communicate in text comments. To do this, you can draw from other books, articles, movies, television shows or your own writing and experience.

So, you and your partner love the show *Firefly*? Find ways to relate a dialogue consistency issue with Captain Mal to find a shiny solution. "You know how Mal speaks in vastly different ways to Kaylee, Inara and Zoe? His character remains consistent, though. I think a *Firefly* binge weekend is in order for us to examine how Joss Whedon accomplishes that. You up for it?"

MEA: Don't underestimate your personal experiences. Sometimes, the solution to your partner's problems is a process you've already vetted in your own work.

Share Reactions When Possible.

A bonus when critiquing that won't take much additional time or effort on your part—but will mean the world to the author—is to share your organic reactions. These additions will let your author know, for example, if he's set the mood he desired, if a joke went over well or if the twist had too much foreshadowing. It's encouraging for the author to know when his written moments hit their intended mark. With this boost tucked away, he can push through the necessary revisions to make his story better. On the flip side, if you're laughing when you should be crying, the author knows where he has work to do.

JOY: It's okay to be vulnerable with your partner. Tell him you bawled at the end of chapter eighteen or couldn't stop laughing when the dragon babies had the hiccups and accidentally burned the bedsheets.

Golden nuggets of reader reaction not only let the writer know he is succeeding in conveying emotions through his words but also help you bond over this story and grow closer in your relationship. Isn't that lovely?

Remain In Your Critique Lane.

MEA: What if you find yourself disagreeing with the author's choices? When your opinion stands against the author's intent or you find yourself creating story elements to make sense of his plot, you're in danger of crossing a critique line. Remember you are the critique partner, not the author. Keep the author's vision in mind as you consider each comment and suggestion—even if you prefer your version of his story better. (Of course you do. They're your ideas.)

Advise within the author's previously discussed boundaries, bearing in mind his story themes and perspectives, and you might surprise yourself at how creative you can get finding solutions to make the story better while maintaining the author's original intent. You may even develop empathy in the process.

JOY: What if the author's story intent doesn't match up with his publishing goals, though? Once again, we call upon the powers of honesty to save your partner's bacon. Stay in your lane as you pull out a map for him to consider alternative routes to his current choices. If your partner doesn't take your advice, it's his future and his story. Your suggestions are valid and may be what you would do, but we are all individuals. Guard yourself from becoming upset if he makes choices outside your presented case.

In order to do this well, you need to honor the writer's identity, theme and publishing goals. View your evaluation through the lens of his perspective, ensuring the story upholds that standard. If he told you his desire is to have this book published by one of the top publishers and you feel that his story is, for example, too niche to land at one of the top houses, be candid with him and help him think through all his options.

MEA: You could share your concerns like this, "As well as you integrated the theme of sacrifice through this story and as well as you achieved an entertaining and engaging story despite my initial uncertainties about the presentation, you may want to reconsider your publishing goals. This might be a tough sell to the big companies we initially discussed. It could also be hard to find an agent willing to take a risk on it. Have you considered some smaller specialty presses? Some of them market to your target audience and would be more likely to want Bosch's story. Just a thought! No matter what you choose, I'll be cheering you all the way through publication."

A little reassurance that you're cool with whatever he chooses and believe in him and his work will open up the space for him to decide without the influence of subconscious pressure.

JOY: You should also retain your focus of what he asked you to do in the first place. A well-meaning critique partner may overwhelm or annoy with too much explanation of why he loved the main character when the author just wants to get to the two sentences on how to fix the gaping plot hole in chapter ten. Be sure to answer the questions you're asked when you critique. Then, gush over your favorite spots.

Break Rules But Do It Well.

MEA: We devoted a bunch of ink back in Chat Two to the basic story knowledge needed to give a critique. You will evaluate your critique partner's success—or lack thereof—by filtering his manuscript through these fundamentals. You should then be able to decipher if the author is using the standards well or if he's breaking them well. Yes, you read that right; you can break the rules, but you've got to do it well.

If the story you're critiquing isn't following structure or character norms, how will you know if it's going well or not? We're assuming at this point, since you're considering writing as a significant part of your life, you have read a multitude of books. Some you flew through, staying up all night because you had to know how things turned out; some you struggled through because, if it ended well, it would be worth the torture; and some you put down because you didn't want to break your e-reader by throwing it against the wall.

JOY: Our first indication if something is working or not is our instinct. If your partner is trying something new and it isn't going well, you'll know because of the lack of emotional fulfillment when you've finished the story or the feelings of confusion, frustration or boredom during the reading. If he's breaking the rules correctly, you might feel a sense of wonder, curiosity and anticipation as you read; and, when you finish, you'll potentially take a deep breath of contentment.

Either way, you must inform your partner of his success or lack thereof. Don't let him throw himself to the wolves of critics and reviewers without first warning him of the raw meat in his coat pockets.

Acknowledge Both Strengths And Weaknesses.

MEA: Keep in mind that every story will have both strengths and weaknesses. A critique partner should never present the bad or the good alone. If you focus only on the bad, your critique is an ambush. If you focus solely on the good, it gives the author an unrealistic view of his abilities. It's the combination of the two—improvement and praise—that gifts your partner the tools and confidence he needs to continue smoothing the rough edges and grow as a writer.

PULL OUT YOUR LAST challenge and add the additions to the QWERTY Critique Truth Bomb Formula:

> **QWERTY Critique Truth Bomb Formula:**
> *Commendation + Opinion + Discussion = Effective*
> *Truth x Specificity = Truth Bomb That Slays*

Does your previous situation lend itself to becoming a Truth Bomb That Slays by adding specific contextual proof or relevant outside examples? Clarity comes through specifics. The idea is that, with your examples, the person to whom you're speaking will better comprehend the message you have crafted. You can be more confident your suggestions were heard; and, from there, your counterpart can choose to alter his situation or not.

Section IV: Contingencies

What If The Story Needs More Help Than You Can Give?

JOY: We get it. We've read those stories that weren't fleshed out yet. We've also been that person who shared pieces before they were ready. Here's the thing: you may come across a manuscript about which you can find absolutely nothing good to say or in which you isolate at least a dozen major issues. Maybe the characters are stereotypical in all the worst possible ways, the dialogue is campy and lacking purpose, there was no clear theme, the ending redeemed nothing and you still don't have a clue what story the author intended to tell. It's rare, but it could happen.

MEA: You should be honest without being unduly harsh. You owe it to your integrity and the author's to do so, but you don't have to continue the relationship if it can't be reciprocal.

Practically, you have a few options. If you're going through this book's interview process alongside this writer, you are probably in the sample stage and have a choice to take it or leave it. You can end it there quickly with a "Thanks, but no thanks," not touching his piece with a critique. Tell the person sooner rather than later, so he can discontinue his critique. If that person has already given you a critique, etiquette calls for reciprocation.

JOY: Another option would be to finish the critique with the main issues in red to help him *without* claiming him as a CP. He made it all the way to the example critique level, so you must have liked him. Your critique can help him see his need, so he can study up on story while searching for a partner on his level. Also, you may consider staying friends in some form or fashion, connected by writing or other commonalities. If he asks you to be his mentor, make sure you have the time for such a commitment. If you don't, kindly decline.

Consider if you know him well enough for your honesty to get more specific. Can you let him know all the issues and concerns you have without ruining your friendship? Would he be receptive to suggestions of writing courses or craft books that helped you? Give him any suggestions you can but be clear about your inability to continue this partnership. If you're unsure of his reaction, you could always ask if he would like resource suggestions to help him reach the next level.

MEA: If you are the person who gets turned down as a critique partner with a "Thanks, but no thanks" message or a critique with no further hope of partnership, it's going to be okay. Keep working on your craft and searching for the right partner. Translate the message received to mean "Not quite yet," focusing on the *yet*.

This is not a personal blow. Who you are—your personality and character—passed the test. Your craft knowledge and implementation need more work. Each writer has to recognize and act upon his needs; and, honestly, that person was probably not who you need at this time either. Joy and I believe you have the ability to learn from the experience and try again to find your partner while refining your craft. Plus, this almost-partner may have given you the equivalent of a syllabus to guide your personal craft course.

JOY: What if you've already made a commitment to a person? Well, that makes it a little more difficult to handle smoothly. The first thing you need to decide is if continuing this partnership is best for you.

If you choose to continue, understand you will be more of his mentor than critique partner. His critiques may be on a lower skill level, but that's not to say they won't hold some value. As he grows in skill and practice, he could become a full-fledged CP. For now, you will be responsible for teaching him, which could result in similar strengths and weaknesses.

Eventually, individual thought will form, and he can become a much-needed writing advisor to you as well. Critique his work and explain the situation honestly. He might choose to find someone on his level, but we believe he will appreciate the appraisal, whether he chooses to hang around or not.

MEA: You could, instead, change his position in your professional life from critique partner to writing friend. Hand him back the critique and ask him to call you after he's had a few days to look over it. Explain that you both need something different than either of you can fulfill.

We know it sounds like a bad breakup; but, if the other person doesn't recognize how you would be sacrificing your writing to boost his, he may not have had the kind of giving spirit needed for a healthy CP relationship.

Your final option is to drop him like a hotcake. Critique his piece and send it back with a kind yet firm email that leaves no room for further collaboration.

JOY: Notice in all these options, we never said to ghost (ignore) anyone. That may be the easiest thing to do, but you're a writer. If you wanted easy, you'd find another passion. Be upstanding. Own the fact that your strengths and weakness do not complement his. Know what you need and honor who you are by standing firm.

Give your almost-partner a parting gift of improvement suggestions. This task returns us to our original conundrum—what do you say when the manuscript has no redeeming qualities?

If you can't find anything word-wise to praise, look outside the page. Is it the author's first completed piece? That's a big deal. Did this person fight tooth and nail to honor his designated writing time? That discipline is honorable, and you should commend him. Is the person's kind personality causing lack of conflict between characters? Praise his inherent characteristic, while reminding him that, like a person needs extra makeup during a photo shoot for the best results, stories require extra meanness toward the characters to spotlight story theme and overall purpose. Unfortunate events produce great stories.

DO YOU HAVE A hard time saying "No" or do you break out in hives at the thought of conflict or presenting a hard truth? This challenge is mostly for you. Understanding that rejections should be decided upon on a case-by-case basis, create a conversational template in case you need to part ways with a potential or current critique partner. Review the options in this section. If none of them feel right, create your own. Having this plan in your back pocket may calm you when struggles arise. Remember, though, some conflicts are worth the effort to mend instead of tear.

SECTION V: EXPECTATIONS

What Should You Expect After You Deliver A Critique?

MEA: You've hit the *send* button on your critique. Your fingers rest for the first time in ages, and your eyes process nature rather than a backlit screen. Your mind hasn't translated a reaction or evaluation into words for at least ten minutes. The quiet causes anxiety to randomly spike. Shouldn't you hear keystrokes?

Congratulations! You're transitioning from *am critiquing* to *have critiqued*. It can sometimes be jarring—especially if you're new to the critiquing world. Expect some lostness between the end of the critique and the moment you remember you have, for example, other projects, a family, a trip or a need for self-care.

JOY: If you send the finished notes through email, you should expect a grateful response acknowledging that your partner has received the package. You may get some random questions or requests for clarification. Your next big interaction with your partner will likely be after he goes through the critique—perhaps a follow-up phone call or two as he dives into revisions, if that's what you agreed to at the beginning. Your early communication should guide your expectations for this stage.

You can expect your partner to buck some of your suggestions. You are a huge part in the development of this work, but you are not its creator. At the end of the day, the author has to make the changes he believes are the best fit for his story and its purpose. If your advice isn't accepted, that doesn't mean he didn't appreciate it or that it wasn't valid or fitting. It simply means the author decided something else was best for his story. In these instances, it is helpful to remember the author often knows things about his characters and topic that aren't on the page.

MEA: Of course, it could also mean he's not willing to let something go. You could have made the best suggestion—one he should have utilized. The final decision is still the author's, but feel free to kindly call him out if you believe he's using the wrong justification for keeping something that doesn't work.

Questions come back into play in this situation. Ask why he wants to stick to his choice. It may be that, as you ask questions, he begins to see things from a different perspective. For a thriving relationship, talk it out so no bitterness can set up shop in either of you. Maybe he needs to understand your perspective, or you need a glimpse at the backstory that will come to light in book two. Have your conversation but don't nag. When it's over, acquiesce if he retains his choice or temper your celebration if your suggestion is adopted. Either way, you've done your best by your partner and now you have your own work to do.

JOY: We had this happen with *Any Good Thing*. One of my characters got ignored through much of my first draft. Mea pointed out all the issues with my choice, but I stubbornly stuck to my guns and defended why I didn't want Jack to reach out to this person sooner.

Mea continued pointing out the downsides to my choice but backed away after making sure she'd articulated her stance with all its supporting reasons. As I plunged further into revisions, I realized Mea was right after all …

MEA: Huzzah!

JOY: ...and discovered additional development benefits to pulling that character further into the story.

MEA: This is the ideal situation—at least for me—but we're all human and, sometimes, can be led by emotions such as pride and jealousy. We may experience complicated situations in our personal lives that make us feel unimportant and out of control of our surroundings. It can be tempting to use confronting conversations to counteract life situations and create a fleeting moment of confidence.

Before you react to your partner's dismissal of your advice, check your motivations. Are they honorable, or could a sucky life situation be pushing you to grasp at the nearest opportunity to control something?

MAKE A LIST OF what you will do after your critique. As soon as the critique has reached your partner, work your list for two reasons. First, you may be worried about how your partner will handle your comments. If you were truthful and tactful, you have nothing to worry about; and the list will distract you from fretting.

Second, you have spent considerable time and effort on someone else. It's now time to give back to your other relationships and yourself. It might be easy to dwell on your advice. *Was it right? Should I have been that honest? Will I still have a CP tomorrow?*

These thoughts can lead to procrastination, and you might neglect your creative endeavors. Hopefully, the list will remind you of your dreams and persuade you to return to the present.

Recap

- Communication is the king of quality critiques. Repetition and clarity result in positive interactions. Well-placed questions can be the best way for your partner to discover hidden depth in his piece.
- The way you phrase your suggestion is just as important as the actual words. Be careful how your words "sound," even through type, and don't forget to sound like YOU.
- Always provide contextual proof or outside examples for big assertions and explain how you've come to that opinion. Specificity yields clarity. Find your focus in the process as you remember the author's intent and voice and seek for the good and bad.

- Take on the challenge of verbalizing any uncomfortable feelings in regards to your partner's piece and finding the words to address them. Your silence could be the downfall of the whole thing. It's okay to end the partnership if it's not emotionally or professionally beneficial for both parties.
- Form realistic expectations of your time after delivering a critique and have an action plan in place to follow.

Receiving a Critique

CHAT SIX:
Receiving a Critique

ANY CRITIQUE—NO MATTER how kind and well-intentioned—will sting. We share our tips for accepting, processing and utilizing a critique to make us better writers with stronger words.

SECTION I: DURING THE CRITIQUE

What Should You Do While You Are Waiting For Your Critique?

JOY: While your critique partner has that literary piece of your heart—and his red pen—your main goal is to not wonder about or work on that particular piece.

I know you just want to move Chapter 4 to Act 3 and, really, the girl's hair should be black with purple stripes instead of purple with black stripes, and the inciting incident doesn't feel inciting enough, and maybe you should just ...

MEA: No.

JOY: Just ... no.

MEA: Separating yourself from the work as much as you can before you get the critique back is going to serve you well. Promise. How about some ideas to keep yourself busy while you wait?

- Work on another creative project.
- You may have swapped projects with your critique partner. If so, get to critiquing your partner's work, Friend!
- Work on business things if you're considering a creative career. You could schedule social media posts for the whole month or write a few blog posts. Research agents or publishing companies. Take marketing classes or learn more about self-publishing. Get a jump on this end, so when your critique comes back, you won't have to split your focus.
- If this is an early work for you, research a revision plan that resonates with you.
- Relax. Your body has been in an L-shape for the last six weeks or more, depending on the length of your project, so maybe remind it what it feels like to make an X? Spell YMCA? Pretend it's a tree?
- Spend time with people other than your characters.

- Get some vitamin D. (That's sunshine, in case you've forgotten.)
- Exercise. Movement is important for creatives whose primary tools are our head and hands. We've got to prioritize our health, especially if writing is a life habit.
- Read—for the fun of it!

JOY: One of the two main reasons we want you to stay busy is this: you absolutely, positively cannot repetitively contact your CP to see how the revisions are going. If he contacts you, you can answer, of course; but you cannot hound your partner for scraps of a critique that will come to you whole in time.

Daily *How's it going? What page are you on? Have you gotten to the part when...* texts are obnoxious. Don't be obnoxious; knit a sweater to keep from bugging him. That way, you'll have a sweater *and* a critique partner once you get your manuscript back!

Our second reason for you to stay busy is in "Section III: Moving On from the Critique."

WRITE DOWN THINGS YOU would like to do while you wait for the return of your critique. Be specific and vary your categories. For example, what would you like to do with someone other than your critique partner? How can you incorporate self-care? Could you begin planning your next project? Have you considered volunteering at an animal shelter? Your writing benefits from life experiences, so go live a little.

Section II: Reviewing The Critique

How Should You Approach Your Initial Review?

MEA: Remind yourself of a few things before opening your critique: Your critique partner is not out to get you. You've carefully chosen this person. He is invested in your success. He's proven himself capable, and you've decided to trust him.

JOY: Know that all critiques assessing a creative endeavor hurt a little. Creative words have tiny threads connected to our souls, and that's what makes your project special, unique and evocative. When a critique comes in, even a healthy one, the suggestions tug on those tiny threads; and the tension smarts.

We want you to know that this feeling is not some cosmic sign that you have picked the wrong person to evaluate your heart projects. You don't necessarily need a new critique partner. Your reaction is only a sign that you care. It's our opinion that caring is necessary to make good art. So, hold fast. You're going to get through this.

MEA: Critiques of your art are not a reflection of how someone feels about you as the artist. Separating your self-identity from your work is imperative to surviving the emotions surrounding creative endeavors. Remember, art is subjective and responses to it are filtered through another person's personality, experience and natural preferences.

Some people will hide your work in their hearts for the rest of their lives, get tattoos to remind them of your words and the emotions they caused, tell their friends you are the best person ever because you made the Thing. But, other people will feel differently and have reactions that are excessive and possibly unfair.

JOY: And, that's okay, too.

One purpose of art is to spread a piece of yourself out into the world. You've done that. Your job is complete. What a person feels or thinks about it doesn't have anything to do with you or your self-worth.

Your writing comes from a place inside you, but no one project can encompass all that you are. The next creative project you set free will be different from the last because you will continue to improve as you practice and learn, and your life perspectives will widen and deepen as your experiences multiply.

MEA: If you followed the processes in this book to connect with a critique partner, we feel confident you'll receive an honest, tactful, educated and kind critique. If it's not, remember again—seriously, it's important enough to repeat—art is subjective and your worth is not decided by someone's evaluation of your work.

JOY: No matter what is on the inside of the document you're about to open, a person—your Person—dedicated time and effort to help you, and you're grateful for that care. Write a thank you note to your critique partner because it's important to acknowledge the effort now instead of after your perusal of their suggestions. You don't want your critique partner sitting in the background wondering if the internet ate the email or if you hate him for his honesty.

We creatives have a healthy imagination. We can mentally "see" our critique partners seething with disdain, whether it's warranted or not. So, thank your CP. Tell him you'll get back to him as soon as you process the comments and give a specific timeline, if possible. Tell him you look forward to critiquing his next project and that the texted picture of the clown decorating the ficus tree was hilarious.

Now, it's time. Open that document.

WRITE A POSITIVE QUOTE and post it somewhere you'll see it as you review your critiqued manuscript. Let it remind you that good things are to come. If you can't think of one, we have some suggestions.

> *All criticism burns. The blister is a sign that you care, and caring is a necessary component of good art.*
> ~ Mea Smith

> *Through a careful un-layering of our writing, we find the precious gems and veins of gold. Put back together without the dirt, our story can finally shine.*
> ~ Joy E. Rancatore

> *My worth doesn't hinge on the response to my art.*
> ~ Mea Smith

Thoroughly critiqued now, my work can stand resolute against critics later.
> ~ Joy E. Rancatore

SECTION III: MOVING ON FROM THE CRITIQUE

You've Read The Comments. Now What?

MEA: You've opened the document and read through the comments, advice, suggestions and commentary. You may be overwhelmed at the revision work ahead of you. You may be overcome by emotions that are outside of your typical, fun-loving demeanor. This is normal. Remember when we warned you early on about feeling protective of your writing?

JOY: So, what do you do with all the feelings? Should you scrap the project and start over? Why is there no ice cream in your house, darn it?

MEA: Okay, first question: you separate and evaluate the emotions. Just like your partner found a way to articulate his thoughts regarding your piece, you need to find a way to articulate your emotions and find out why you feel them. Are they justified or are they reactionary? You can decide what to do with them once you determine if they are legitimate or not.

JOY: Next question: please—we beg you—do not throw your project away; you'll regret it. The purpose of a critique is to find ways to improve a piece. Your partner can't do that if he doesn't pick things apart and tell you about his findings. What you have in your hands is not a manuscript covered in blood spots, but rather a manuscript dappled with rubies. These gems are the key to make your piece sharable, publishable even. Polishing them can help clearly share your message.

And, you asked him to help you. Don't forget that. You really did want this—and you will again, once you sift through your initial emotions.

MEA: Finally, the ice cream: you didn't go to the store and need to rectify this immediately. While you're out, we have specific tastes—Blue Bell Camo 'n Cream and Raspberry Fudge Brownie. Please, and thank you!

JOY: We want to remind you, in the midst of all the emotions, to not act on impulse. You cannot punch your critique partner. It's called assault, and you will be arrested. Remember how we told you our creative work is connected to our souls and how even healthy critiques can hurt? Pull those truths to the forefront of your mind, close your eyes and take deep breaths. That's it. Much better.

MEA: First viewings of critiques tend to bruise our pride. No contacting your critique partner, terminating friendships or insulting his mom while you're in this state. Remember, you care for him. You've forged this relationship to go beyond critiques, in some cases. You'll regret a rash decision later, and it's incredibly difficult to come back from mistakes like that.

JOY: Please keep one other thing in mind: if your desire is to publish, thousands of reader reviews are in your future. These people don't know your main character is a memorial to your sister or the bullying scene is straight out of your past—a past you've worked for decades to overcome. And, get ready for another truth bomb. Those readers may not simply review or critique; they may criticize and attack both the words and the wordsmith.

Here is the beauty in this grenade-like truth: you've carefully chosen a critique partner who might know those personal details, if you've shared them. He cares about your scars and will be sensitive to the facts in your fiction or nonfiction. More than that? He cares about you, your work and your success. His critique might sting, but it's there to prepare you for your post-publication future. With his help—along with the help of editors, beta readers, publishers and your entire literary team—your work will become the best representation of the story you wanted to tell and you'll become the seasoned, mature author you were created to be.

So, when the haters come—and, they will—you'll have an entire entourage of people, including your CP, to lean on, with the knowledge they saw your words' worth and gave their all to help you make them sparkle.

MEA: We have a few suggestions to get you from "My eyes! My eyes! Too much red!" to "Let's fix this thing!"

TAKE A BEAT.

Let the critique marinate for a day or two. Then, make one of his suggested changes. It's better, right? When you glimpse a shimmer of the overall piece after revision, excitement replaces negative reactions, and you'll be ready to work. At this point, open the document again and see what other sparkling improvements it contains.

Look At Your Project From A Different Perspective.

JOY: Ready for our promised second reason for separating yourself from your work while your partner is critiquing? You've been away from the work since your CP received it, which should make it easier for you to imagine you aren't the author ... just another person working to make the theme and story shine.

Stepping back and looking at your piece as a reader or as one who's critiquing can help you keep the creator emotions and attachments at bay. Those buggers stunt new ideas from forming, and they inundate you with memories of the good times you and—for example—an unnecessary, but lovable, character had together.

They reinstate the past pride you had when you found just the right word to express your intention in the sentence you now have to delete. They make you hesitate doing a thing your logic knows is right. The emotions and attachments like the project the way it is, and you can't convince them that you can make it better. Your sentiments cling to the things you've got to cut or change like the lovies or binkies or pacifiers they are. (We're both moms; you knew we were going to have a baby reference in here somewhere.)

MEA: You have to distance yourself from the story to calm those emotions and make clear and necessary decisions in a timely manner. Otherwise, you'll be hemming and hawing through your entire revision, and the results will be an incohesive unfinished product that reflects your indecision.

An interesting benefit of changing your perspective is a reactivation of your right brain concerning this story. It thought it was done with these characters, but you've shown it an angle it hasn't seen before. Combine that with your CP's guiding questions sprinkled through his critique, and your creative side just discovered an addition to the playground it thought it had exhausted. It's ready to discover new things about the characters and unknown plot details. Things are about to get crazy cool.

WRITE DOWN ANY QUESTIONS.

JOY: As you examine your CP's comments, you'll have clarifying questions that require answers. Note the location of the comment by the question, too, especially if it's a large project. Once all of your questions are written down, schedule a time to contact your CP, if you haven't done so already. If you're talking in person or on the phone, honor your CP's time (and your own) by being prepared. Readiness ensures you get all your questions out there and possibly answered in one go. If you're contacting him through email, compile and proof your questions for clarity and clean writing. Press *send*.

MEA: After that conversation or written communication, if you need clarification on an answer, ask your CP again. Don't brood over it and become a bitter lemon. He can't read your mind and doesn't know you're unsure of exactly what he meant. Your disappointment will be your fault (not your critique partner's) if you don't reach out and ask. The bitterness and disappointment you harbor will negatively affect the professional and personal relationship you have so carefully cultivated, so keep your lines of communication open and confusion free.

Discuss Disagreements In A Productive Manner.

JOY: If he makes a suggestion you don't agree with, discuss it, explaining your reasoning for disagreeing. He may simply say, "Okay—your story!" and move on to the next thing. Or, he might pause, consider your opinion and respond with another reason to support his suggestions. This is good. You're having a healthy debate. That's high-level communication, Friend!

MEA: Make sure you're carefully listening and seriously considering his points. If your critique partner brings up an issue for discussion, remember he is looking out for you and your story's best interest. His name isn't on the piece, so no overt personal benefit comes from him countering your choice. It's just plain easier to remain silent; so, if your partner decides to fight a battle, it's most likely for your glory. Take time before you completely reject or accept it. You don't want to be too hasty either way. Mull it over—clarity may come with time and careful consideration. His suggestion could very well be the piece that makes your entire story move more smoothly.

JOY: However, because we're imperfect humans, his reasoning could be warped. So, if his motives seem flawed and out of character, it's okay to ask what is really going on and how you can help. This is the friend side of your partnership.

Either way, talk it out. We're proud of your mad communication skills.

MEA: Keep in mind as you move forward that you'll receive a comparative amount to what you put in. If you dial it in and don't give your all to your partner while critiquing his book, he is unlikely to give more attention to yours. Likewise, if you don't graciously accept his critique, strongly consider his suggestions and utilize the ones that best fit to improve your work, he is not likely to be as thorough and generous in the future when he realizes you're ignoring him. Please don't sabotage yourself, your art or your relationship.

Well, Friend, you're ready to move forward. Plan a strategy to make your revisions and begin. Check our QWERTY recommendations in Appendix I for resources to help you do that ... or ask your CP for suggestions!

RECOGNIZE THE EMOTIONAL ANGST you experienced in accepting this critique of your work and journal candidly about your reactions. Revisit your purpose in writing and remind yourself of your goals. How will this critique—and the many more to come—help you attain your dreams and fulfill your purpose?

Go through the critique again. List repetitive issues you need to address during revisions. We speak from experience—having this list nearby during revisions will help you focus when all the words begin to blur.

Recap

- Taking your mind off your submitted work while it's being critiqued may be the best thing you can do for your current piece.

- Once you receive the critique, remember your critique partner has your best interests in mind and his main goal is to help you succeed.
- Take the time necessary to process your emotions after receiving your critique. Don't make any big decisions until those strong reactions have cooled.
- Embrace the opportunity to improve your manuscript. Ask your partner clarifying questions and discuss differences in opinion. Make a plan and begin revisions.

Conclusion

JOY: You've made it through, Friend! You've identified your need for a critique partner, done the necessary self-evaluation to be a good one, gone through the steps to finding one or more and experienced at least a practice round of critiques.

You rock ice for real!

MEA: You're the bomb!

JOY: Seriously, we are so proud of you! Can we all go out for tacos together to celebrate? We're not joking. We truly, madly, deeply love tacos. And, not just on Tuesdays.

MEA: As that request is highly impractical, we'll have to settle with wrapping this conversation up in a way that keeps you moving forward in your partnership.

Always Respect Each Other, Even When It's Hard.

We caution you to keep one thing in mind: you will not always agree. And, that's okay! Just be sure you've communicated clearly and let go of whatever it is you don't agree on. Listen. Articulate your opinion. Respect each other. Move on.

Keep Up The Good Communication Work!

JOY: Communication, more than any other aspect of your relationship, remains vitally important from start to finish and back through again. Keep talking. Keep encouraging. Keep evaluating your work, your expectations, your needs, your goals and your partnership. These are ever-changing because we are ever-changing.

Discuss An *Out Clause.*

MEA: Throughout this book, we've told you how to keep your critique partnership. Now, we have to address how to end it, because that's the responsible thing to do, right? We hope you never have to use it; but, if you are of the anti-drama mentality, it may calm you to have proactively discussed an *Out Clause* and when it should be used. Life situations change; availability changes; people change. Plan ahead and set yourselves up for a continuation of your friendship even if your critique partnership cannot. The two of you may decide at the beginning to either discuss this possibility or put things in writing—a pact of sorts.

JOY: We have developed a Critique Partner Contract for you to use or adapt. It includes a written *Out Clause*. You'll find it in Appendix J. Whether you get that official or not, should the need arise to part ways, be honest— another QWERTY motto on repeat. Let your partner know right away if something has changed and you're no longer able to continue. Complete promised critiquing, if possible, and discuss your availability for future clarifications on past projects.

This need may arise for a variety of reasons. A new job may require you to set your publication goals aside for a while. You might have a new baby or find yourself as a primary caretaker to a parent or spouse. You may even decide you cannot continue as a writer. Your abilities as writers could progress at different rates and no longer line up on the same experience and knowledge levels. A new genre focus could no longer fit your partner's approved categories.

Whatever the case, it is okay for you to move on. Of course, we want you to stay together forever, but sometimes that's just not in the cards. This precaution is to hopefully salvage your friendship after the critiquing partnership has ended.

MEA: Find other ways to support one another. Perhaps you could be an occasional beta reader? Maybe join his launch team? Maybe just cheer one another on through whatever comes. At the very least, our desire is that you have developed a friendship that will continue beyond the final critique.

Maintain Your Friendship.

Remember that saying from when we were kids (or *The Shining*), "All work and no play makes Jack a dull boy?" Well, it applies here. You cannot be all about the work and the craft and the evaluations all the time and expect to develop and maintain a friendship. As hard as it might be for some of us, we encourage you to take a break and have fun together!

JOY: While we wrote the first draft of this book, we took breaks to laugh and joke and eat and swim. We talked over memories and shared favorite scenes from books and movies and chatted about our favorite writers and podcasts. We do the same when we discuss each other's critiques or have a brainstorming session. When we podcast together, we take the time to catch up on each other's week, share any big news and otherwise engage with each other before we hit record. And, you know what else we do?

We go out for tacos!

MEA: If you're in this for keeps, your partner may be your lifesaver on occasion. And, you may be his. Comfort comes from knowing someone has your back. It encourages you to step into the unknown, take risks and try something new.

QWERTYS: Ask. Us. How. We. Know.

QWERTY FRIENDS

QWERTY Friends

WE INVITED SEVERAL AUTHORS to share their critique partner stories in this book. The following pages provide you a glimpse behind the scenes into what this type of writing relationship can look like.

We gave each of them a series of background questions to answer. Most of those were the same, but we did ask each group one focus question specific to their situation. You will see similarities as well as differences. You will also discover a few of our tips in action through these partners' processes.

Ready to be inspired? Read on!

Candice Marley Conner & Carrie Dalby

Focus Question: Is it difficult for you to critique each other's work since you write in different genres? And, how do you make it work?

CANDICE: It's not difficult to critique each other's work, and the short answer is that we make it work because we're both so widely read.

While Carrie writes adult Southern Gothic family sagas and I write picture books to young adult, we both thoroughly know what's expected out of the different age groups and genres. My middle grade and young adult usually have southern gothic elements woven in so it's not too different, like high fantasy to contemporary would be. Sometimes I'm not her target audience for the romantic scenes, but I can still read for pacing, mood, character believability, and line edits.

CARRIE: Though my current project is a book series for adult readers, my literary journey began with upper middle grade/young adult, and it will always be my first love. I'm a former children's book specialist at a large book store chain, and my first two novels are for preteens to teens. Having a critique partner who loves and respects the genre you work in is key—THE key. You don't have to write the same things, just be well-read in the represented genres.

About ten years ago, I was in a critique group with a mix of writers, including some who didn't read (and at least one who looked down on) YA literature. It didn't work out well to only receive half the functional input that the other members were getting out of the meetings because of the reader gap. Fortunately, another member writing YA pulled out, and we created our own group with other local writers who were working on YA projects at the time. From there, the membership has changed a bit and some of the members switched age genres—some dipping into middle grade and picture books (like Candice) and others (like me) branching into adult—but we all respect and read the different genres.

How did you meet?

CANDICE: Both being members of the Mobile Writers' Guild, Carrie offered to beta read a YA manuscript I was working on. At that time (around 2012), I was at a complete loss of how to find beta readers or critique partners. Only my mom and best friend had read it, and I didn't know where to go from there. A couple years later when [Carrie's] critique group, Write Club, had a vacancy, they invited me to join.

CARRIE: We met through Mobile Writers' Guild, a group in the Mobile Bay Area for authors of all genres/forms at every level of the journey to publication. We meet monthly September to May at one of the library branches. It's been central on my journey for networking and expanding my knowledge.

What has been the greatest benefit of your partnership?

CANDICE: Meeting in person. Online critique groups are wonderful, but there's just something about being across the table from someone and being able to ask them tons of questions you might filter out. You never know when the organic-ness of a conversation might lead to a brainstorm.

We also get each other's writing style which is a TREMENDOUS thing. I've received critiques before where it was obvious the person didn't get what I was trying to do with the story. That can be dangerous to voice, the manuscript, and to writing self-confidence. Trust is a big deal.

Also—we carpool to different events! Literary festivals, etc. aren't quite so nerve-wracking when you arrive with a friend you can talk books with.

CARRIE: I'd say friendship. Besides the monthly MWG meetings and numerous text/online messages, we consistently hang out every other week. Granted the critique meeting flows from casual to professional any given minute, in Candice I have a ready friend who completely understands the ups and downs of a writing life—especially while juggling family responsibilities. Another benefit for me (because yes, I've been obsessed with *The Possession Chronicles* for four years now) since I'm working on a series, Candice knows the characters. Even though she's read the most out of anyone, she hasn't read all the stories yet; but I can turn to her when my characters are misbehaving in a different project, and she'll understand.

What has been the greatest challenge of your partnership?

CANDICE: Our critique group actually has five members in it. Unfortunately, everyone is so busy with life and other writing projects, it's hard to carve out face-to-face time with the whole group. Carrie has what she calls Dial-A-Nerd and I have what I call Grammar-

Phone, so anytime any of us are stumped or need a confidence booster, help is just a group message away.

CARRIE: As Candice mentioned, we're only two in a larger critique group, but out of the last year, we've been the consistent ones for the meetings. I don't feel like our partnership is challenged—even as part of the bigger circle. I know they've all got my back, so to speak, with or without exchanging pages on a regular basis.

What do you wish you would have known before you got started?

CANDICE: Hmmm ... I started to say how much patience is necessary; but I think if I knew that before getting serious about writing, I may never have begun! Probably that I wish I knew how important community is to writing. I was pretty isolated in my writing for years before I ventured out into the literary world. It's such a glorious, generous, and incredibly helpful place!

CARRIE: I'm one of those who think "everything happens for a reason," so even my not-perfect experience with the first critique group I was in taught me something. I wouldn't trade anything, except maybe seeking out a writers group sooner. It really helps me keep accountable to myself to know I'll be seeing other people regularly who want to know what I've been doing.

How does your partnership better your writing craft?

CANDICE: I can't submit anything—from magazine poem to novel manuscript—without more eyes on it. Just because I understand what I write, it might not read the same way as I intend; and that's where good critique partners are invaluable. They'll keep you from looking too foolish in front of editors and agents.

CARRIE: It's incredibly helpful for me to have early readers catching everything from grammar/typo issues—I have dyslexic tendencies—to pointing out my often awkward phrasing. I'm a very visual person and sometimes my descriptions overwhelm readers, so my CP helps me learn when I go too far with my details. Candice (and the group at large) is great at pointing out the good in each other's writing. Knowing I've got characterization down or evoke emotions in the reader helps me gain the confidence to keep at it despite my shortcomings, rejections, or bad reviews.

Tell us about your critique process.

CANDICE: We meet every other week to trade critique notes. What we share depends on the project. The last thing I sent Carrie was a middle grade short story for a magazine call for submissions. Since it was around 1,200 words, I emailed her the whole story so she could read it ahead of time, make notes, and we could discuss them in-person that week. Before that was a chapter book that I sent two chapters at a time since I was writing it as we went along. Knowing we would meet kept me writing a minimum a chapter a week, which was good encouragement. I tend to jump around on my projects when I'm not in the throes of a middle grade or YA novel, while Carrie is possessed with *The Possession Chronicles*.

CARRIE: We meet every other week. Our deadline is the weekend before the mid-week meeting. We used to have a ten-page limit, but as our membership shrunk for the regular meetings, we've increased the page count. We officially stretched to fifteen pages, but then I got a little crazy and pushed that when my chapters ran long. Candice has been generous with allowing me to send more since it's just the two of us for the time being and I have a backlog of novels and shorter projects waiting to be read—yes, all relating to *The Possession Chronicles*.

We print each other's pages and write notes/edit directly on the page. I use purple ink, and Candice a pencil. When we meet together, we talk it through page by page. Often other ideas come to us, and we discuss them then. Each member in the group has different strengths. While I mark things I catch, I'm not great at spelling or grammar. For example, my motto with commas is, "When in doubt, leave it out," which makes for a lot of added commas for my critique partner—and editor. I am good at catching redundancies, marking phrases that trip me up as a reader, pacing, character stability (even when they're unstable), and making sure the story circles back to an idea first introduced in the beginning.

About the Partners

Growing up between swamps, a river, and the Gulf Coast, **CANDICE MARLEY CONNER's** stories emerge from gnarled burrows, muddy water, and salty air. The kidlit haint at a local indie bookstore, The Haunted Bookshop, she is also a Local Liaison and PAL member of SCBWI and an officer for the Mobile Writers' Guild. Her debut picture book, *Sassafras and her Teeny Tiny Tail*, is forthcoming winter of 2019 and her YA Southern mystery, *The Existence of Bea Pearl*, releases Fall 2020. Candice's short stories, poetry, and personal essays are published in various anthologies, including *Mardi Gras Pieces: A Mobile Writers' Guild Anthology*, Owl Hollow Press' *Under the Full Moon's Light*, Chicken Soup for the Soul, and *Fireflies & Fairy Dust: A Fantasy Anthology*. She enjoys Mardi Gras parades, exploring the Mobile delta, and Taco Tuesdays.

Visit Candice:

www.candicemarleyconner.com
www.twitter.com/Candice_marleyc
www.facebook.com/CMarleyConnerAuthor
www.instagram.com/candice_marleyconner/

CARRIE DALBY, a California native, has lived in Mobile, Alabama, since 1996. Carrie's two young adult novels are *Corroded* and *Fortitude*. *Fortitude* is listed as a "Best History Book for Kids" by Grateful American Foundation, for its historical accuracy and being an engaging read for fifth through tenth graders. Her current project is a historical Southern Gothic family saga for adults, *The Possession Chronicles*. The first three books in the series released during 2019 from Bienvenue Press with more to follow in 2020 and beyond. Beside books, Carrie has published several non-fiction articles in national and international magazines, served two terms as president of Mobile Writers Guild, worked as the Mobile area Local Liaison for SCBWI from 2012-2017, and volunteers with Metro Mobile Literacy Council's annual Young Author events whenever possible. When she's not reading, writing, browsing bookstores and libraries, or homeschooling, Carrie can often be found knitting or attending concerts.

Visit Carrie:
www.carriedalby.com
www.twitter.com/wonderwegian
www.facebook.com/CarrieDalbyAuthor/
www.pinterest.com/wonderwegian/
www.goodreads.com/author/show/14682659.Carrie_Dalby

Karen Hugg & Natasha Oliver

Focus Question: Would you share with us how your critiquing plans for your debut novels didn't come together exactly as you planned and how you decided to continue with your partnership for future pieces?

KAREN: Well, we've never had concrete plans except to share our work whenever needed. That's been going on for almost ten years. Wow! A few years ago, when my kids were in the higher grades of school and I wasn't as busy with my gardening business, I gained a lot of writing time. That's when I wrote *The Forgetting Flower*.

Meanwhile, Natasha was working an editorial job and raising two little girls in a foreign country. And anyone who's a mom knows that when kids are little, that's the most demanding time of childrearing. And the most stressful. So, between raising kids and working and keeping a marriage going, she didn't have the time or quiet space to read *The Forgetting Flower* in full and give feedback, only parts, but that was okay. And when she *did* have bits of time, she was writing *The Evolved Ones*. So, for our debut novels, we weren't exactly aligned in terms of time to read each other's work, but we've done it when we can.

Earlier this year, Natasha moved to England, and everything changed for the better. She's writing full time in what looks to be a comfy house with a big yard and has the support of her in-laws to help with the girls. And because we both, by coincidence, debuted novels this year, we're in closer touch than ever. Now, we support each other through totally different worries!

NATASHA: I met Karen back in graduate school, and we kept in touch because we both respected one another's writing as well as loving each other's personalities. We have shared bits of our work off and on over the years, and while we never formulated a formal critique partner relationship, I think we knew one another well enough to know that we were in fact that, critique partners.

I was so excited and honored when Karen reached out to me to review her manuscript, and I honestly tried to make time for it. It shames me in ways that only another writer can understand that sadly, my life was simply too hectic at the time, which left me with a choice to make: skim over her manuscript and give her vapid feedback just to tick a box or give her manuscript the time and attention it deserved and provide meaningful feedback (even if it wasn't for the entire manuscript).

She is a working mother, a wife, and a writer herself, and so she fully understood that time was something that all too often got away from us. But it still sucked, and I still feel bad about it.

I thought about asking her to read mine when I was done about six months to a year later, but I'd rather we restarted our manuscript-sharing relationship on level ground, on our next books with the understanding that when she asks me to read again, I'd make time for it.

How did you meet?

KAREN: Natasha and I met through the Goddard College MFA program in Port Townsend, Washington. We were attending the bi-annual residency there and hit it off. While that program is for literary writers, it's also open to writers who focus on plot as well. Natasha and I were two of those writers who believed that literary novels could also contain compelling plots. We both wanted to entertain while creating deeper meaning through our stories. We clicked on that aim. At the time, she was writing a fantasy called *Blood Rain*; and I was writing a thriller called *Unearthing Eleven Seconds*, both of which are unpublished and both of which I hope we return to someday.

NATASHA: What Karen said!

WHAT HAS BEEN THE GREATEST BENEFIT OF YOUR PARTNERSHIP?

KAREN: Having a warm, intelligent counterpart who thinks similarly but has her own insights. Our personalities are alike. We're both straightforward, sort of can-do people. Our work ethic and values are similar too. Natasha can be no-nonsense in giving feedback but also generous with her praise. I love that. I crave authenticity and honesty in people, and she's full of it. So, when she reads my stories, it's as if I'm getting a mirrored perspective but with insights I've never thought of. It's brilliant. Her advice, whether about my writing or career or personal life, stays with me after we've talked. So, I'd say having a friend who's in a similar place in life and understands me and believes in me is the greatest benefit. I feel like I can survive this crazy world of writing and publishing books.

NATASHA: That Karen is more than a CP, but a friend; and it's because of that friendship I know her feedback is given with love and support. Karen's smart and she's tenacious as well as caring and honest. Those are traits that are hard to find in a friend, so when you find that in a writer friend, well, you hold on just a bit tighter.

I've been feeling quite vulnerable with the publishing experience, but then having Karen, who's gone through it a few months ahead of me, has been a gift from the universe. She gets me—the writer as well as the woman—and that means she's able to see my writing from a different angle. She can see what I'm trying to achieve and then can comment on whether I actually pulled it off or need to try again.

What Has Been the Greatest Challenge of Your Partnership?

KAREN: What I mentioned above about our lack of time—and proximity. Motherhood is demanding and exhausting. Plus, for several years, she lived in Singapore, and I lived in Seattle. That can be tricky to coordinate! Singapore is fifteen hours ahead of Seattle, or nine hours behind, tomorrow. Did you get that? Neither do I exactly. So, I was overjoyed when she and her family moved to England. Now I know I need to text her before 2:00 p.m. if I want a reply.

NATASHA: Time zones and parenting. While there's no question that we love our children without limit, the truth is those little people can be truly demanding. Karen's three children are older than mine, and therefore, she's had to wait until I "caught up." But we've finally gotten there. I love that she and I can chat daily now, about writing and about life and parenting.

HOW DOES YOUR PARTNERSHIP BETTER YOUR WRITING CRAFT?

KAREN: My craft becomes better because my work is exposed to her unique perspective. The cool thing is we're not identical writers. She's more of a fantasy/Sci-Fi writer, and I'm more literary/mystery inclined. My work is probably a slower read. But what's lovely is she knows that and respects that, and I know her stories move faster and I respect that. We're not out to mold each other into the writers *we'd* be but rather approach the work for what the other wants it to be.

NATASHA: Karen reminds me of the beauty of word choice. She slows me down, and this is critical to my writing. My natural inclination is to go from plot point to plot point, to discuss *what* happens. But when I read Karen's work, I remember the *why* is so very important for the reader to fully understanding the character.

She probably doesn't know this, but her thesis from graduate school, *Unearthing Eleven Seconds*, showed me how to build tension and create intrigue through word choice.

And when I write, even though our genres are different, I want her to respect what I put on the page because her opinion matters. So, she makes me work harder simply by knowing that she's going to read what I've written.

WHAT DOES YOUR CRITIQUE PROCESS LOOK LIKE?

KAREN: First, I should say we're at similar points as writers in that neither of us needs line editing. And now we both work in terms of publication deadlines. So, though we used to send chapters, I think now we'll be sending halves or whole drafts at a time.

Overall, we look at bigger picture issues: how the book flows, logic in plot, character psychology, situational realism, etc. Our sequence is simply to send the manuscript with questions if any, propose a return deadline, and take it from there. We then send feedback emails with lists of questions/issues we think the manuscript needs. She'll tell me what didn't work for her and vice versa. We don't go into too much detail, just outline the major points. It's always exciting to see what the other creates!

NATASHA: I've a good relationship with Karen, and so I can just say to her, "All feedback welcomed." I know that she'll send me her honest thoughts in a manner that's uplifting as well as informative.

When we were in grad school it was chapter based, but now it's like she said: entire manuscripts or sections of the book.

The feedback I get is great because she shows me things about my writing that I'd never see on my own.

About the Partners

KAREN HUGG writes literary mysteries and thrillers inspired by plants. Her stories are set in worlds where plants, real or imagined, affect people in strange new ways. Born and raised in Chicago, she moved to Seattle and worked as an editor before becoming an ornamental horticulturalist and master pruner. She earned her MFA from Goddard College and has been published in the *Rooted* anthology and other publications. When not writing, she digs in the dirt. When not digging in the dirt, she hangs out with her husband, three children, and four pets. When not doing any of those things, she sits outside and stares at the sky.

Visit Karen:

www.karenhugg.com
www.twitter.com/karenhugg
www.facebook.com/karenkhugg
www.instagram.com/karenhugg

NATASHA OLIVER writes strong women of colour characters who are reflective of the female journey. She is the author of the newly released *The Evolved Ones* urban fantasy trilogy. She has an MFA in Creative Writing and has lived in New York, Washington DC, Tokyo, Singapore, and England.

Visit Natasha:
www.natashaoliver.com
www.facebook.com/natashaoliverauthor/
www.instagram.com/natasha_oliver_author/
www.medium.com/@natashaoliver

Autumn Lindsey & Amanda Linsmeier

Focus Question: How do you support one another when the critiquing and revising is done?

AUTUMN: I would say, the majority of the time it looks like sharing things on Pinterest that remind us of each other's works and chatting through Instagram.

AMANDA: I think we're lucky to not only be critique partners but to be friends as well. We talk at least every couple of days, checking in on general life things, mom stuff, and of course, chatting about vampires and coffee!

I think Autumn is such an encouraging light in my life, always cheering me on, from when I was drafting to when I was querying to when I got my agent. She's someone I can count on when I need support, and I hope she feels the same. I was so proud of her when she got her book published, and it's been amazing watching her grow as a writer. I can't wait to see what comes next!

I admit, I can be pushy about writing, and I know other writing friends who might say that. I'm always checking in. *How are your pages coming? Did you figure out that scene you were struggling with? How are submissions going? When are you sending me more?* Etc. I'm just really selfish and want the talented writers I know to finish their stories already so I can read them!

Plus, I really, really love talking about writing (and, you know, writing itself) and encouraging people to push past those tough spots. So, I'm always there to talk writing, publishing, anything.

How did you meet?

AUTUMN: Even though it wasn't that long ago, I really had trouble pinpointing exactly when/how I met Amanda. I'm pretty sure I met her though Writer Moms Inc. We were fast becoming friends through all our fun Instagram chats before she asked if I would be interested in being part of a critique group. Of course, I said, YES! Due to that fact that Amanda's writing is incredibly poetic and dark and filled with beautiful imagery, I was super excited to work with her on a critiquing level. This was my first experience working in a critique group and both Amanda and Kelly taught me SO much on how to give critique as well as take it!

AMANDA: We had a good laugh about this, because neither of us remember exactly how or when we met! We know we've been close for about a year, but we both say we feel like we've known each other forever. I kind of suspect I found Autumn through Writer Moms Inc., either on Facebook or Instagram, and I probably followed her right away, because her feed is gorgeous and she's super fun!

What has been the greatest benefit of your partnership?

AUTUMN: Amanda is someone I can trust fully with my words. So it has been so much fun having someone I can throw out my story ideas to. I know if there is something not working in my story, she won't hesitate to let me know in the kindest and most helpful ways!

AMANDA: Besides becoming friends, I think it's just that I have someone I truly trust with my work. I know she respects it, and she enjoys reading my stories. Plus, we laugh a lot. There are GIFs involved.

What has been the greatest challenge of your partnership?

AUTUMN: The greatest challenge of our partnership is that we live so far away. Amanda is someone I'd love to sit down in a cozy coffee shop and talk about books, and story, and life with. Maybe someday!

AMANDA: I don't know if it's really a challenge, but having a less structured deal than my past critique partnerships/groups took getting used to. I liked having a group in town where I knew we met on x day at x time, and I had to get my work done by then. But we're in totally different states, we're both busy mamas, and generally have all kinds of OTHER things going on, so at this point in our lives, unstructured works.

The great thing is, Autumn is always willing to read, even if we don't have a schedule, so we just take things on an as-needed basis. I do like that I don't feel pressured to send something if it's not ready for another person's eyes yet, and I love knowing that when one of us needs the other's opinion, we're there for it.

WHAT DO YOU WISH YOU WOULD HAVE KNOWN BEFORE YOU GOT STARTED?

AUTUMN: Since working with Amanda was my first experience being a part of a critique group, there isn't anything I wish I knew beforehand. All I can say is getting to know Amanda has made me wish I had a teleporter so we could hang out in person!

AMANDA: How cool Autumn is, and how mad I'd be that we can't hang out in real life.

How Does Your Partnership Better Your Writing Craft?

AUTUMN: I deeply admire Amanda's work and just knowing her helps me feel like a better writer. She has a gift for seeing the heart of a story. She is so encouraging with her critique, and when you ask her to be nitpicky she doesn't hesitate to tell you what you need to hear. I truly appreciate her!

AMANDA: I think, for me, I have to know if there's something positive my partner has found in my work, because even if it's one small thing (and there are a billion critiques) I will cling to that one thing to boost my confidence and carry on, especially when the story gets tough.

Autumn is spectacular about finding something positive to root me, and her suggestions are smart, yet gentle. She will 100 percent mention something that isn't working for her, but she does so in a way that doesn't make me feel like it's total trash. I can fix what needs fixing and then go from there. I also think she's helped draw out my scary, thriller side a little more. We talk about creepy stuff sometimes, and I loved when parts of her story scared me!

WHAT IS A SUMMARY OF YOUR CRITIQUE PROCESS?

AUTUMN: We don't really have a process. Usually it looks like this: I get a message from Amanda saying, "When you get a chance can you read *fill-in-the-blank?* To which I always say, "YES!" because her writing is seriously amazing. When we do trade work for more serious critique, we use track changes in Word to share notes, make corrections and suggestions.

AMANDA: We usually touch base via Instagram DM. I might say, "Hey! Do you have time to read a chapter in the next couple days?" And she'll be all, "Of course! Send away!" and then I'll email it over, and she'll give me feedback either in the document (if we're doing track changes) or just in the DM. It just depends on what stage of the process we're both in.

Sometimes we need in-depth, nitpicky stuff, other times it's simply a, "Can you give me your general thoughts on this opening paragraph so I know I'm on the right track?" kind of thing. She recently read my entire manuscript, and it was nerve-racking but also exciting, waiting on her feedback. When I saw the kind things she had to say, I screenshotted them! She's the best.

About the Partners

AUTUMN LINDSEY lives with her husband and three kids in a deep, dark, magical forest. Fluent in typo and fueled by caffeine, she writes Women's Fiction with characters that bite. You can usually find her lost somewhere in her jungle of a house due to her massive collection of houseplants. Autumn is the author of *Remaining Aileen* and co-founder of Writer Moms Inc.

Visit Autumn:

www.autumnlindsey.com
www.facebook.com/autumnlindseyauthor
www.twitter.com/a_lindseybooks
www.instagram.com/autumnlindseyauthor/

AMANDA LINSMEIER is the author of two poetry books, *Like Waves* and *Our Wild Magic*. Her work has been featured in Moonchild Magazine, Feminine Collective, Kingdoms in the Wild, and more. On the fiction side,  she's at work on more than one dark fairytale retelling. When she's not writing magical things fueled by lots of iced coffee and background music, she works part-time at her local library and brings home more books than she has time to read, but at least she tries. She's the kind of monster who dog-ears book pages, and has read her favorite book, *Beauty* by Robin McKinley, probably a hundred times. Amanda lives in a small house in the woods, with her family, two dogs, and a half-wild cat. She loves sushi, tattoos, fashion, and pretty much anything French.

Visit Amanda:
www.amandalinsmeier.com
www.twitter.com/amandalinsmeier
www.pinterest.com/amandalinsmeier/
www.facebook.com/authoramandalinsmeier
www.instagram.com/amandalinsmeier/

Jamie Raintree & Aimie Runyan

Focus Question: How did your support of one another lead you all the way to obtaining agents and publishers?

JAMIE: Aimie's support has been invaluable in obtaining an agent and publisher. I don't think I would be where I am in my publishing career without her—truly! We actually landed agents within months of each other and have been growing steadily in our careers right alongside each other since then.

The emotional support has probably been the most valuable part of our friendship, but also being able to share resources, discuss industry intel, keep a fire under each other's butts, and cheer each other on every step of the way. Aimie and I are both determined women and having someone as serious as I am about being a published author made me feel so much stronger and more capable in making it happen and sticking with it. I know we both have long careers ahead of us and I look forward to continuing to share the journey with her!

AIMIE: Jamie and I met when we were at very similar stages in our careers. We both had finished manuscripts in good shape and were ready to see how the industry would respond to our work. We hadn't queried yet; and, in my case, no serious writers had yet to critique my manuscript. We started at ground zero together. We read each other's queries and manuscripts, compared notes on prospective agents, boosted signals during Twitter contests, and provided comfort and cheerleading as needed.

How did you meet?

JAMIE: Aimie and I met at the Rocky Mountain Fiction Writers Colorado Gold Conference. Interestingly enough, we sat next to each other at a workshop about creating critique groups. (I purposefully sat next to her because I could tell she was my people.) We struck up a conversation about our kids as we waited for the workshop to start and by the end of the workshop, I had a good feeling about her. So I leaned over and asked her if she wanted to be my critique partner, and she said, "Yes!"

AIMIE: Jamie sat next to me at a panel on the "care and feeding of online critique groups." She handed me a business card and informed me that we were friends now. I was cool with it—best thing that happened to me at an already stellar conference. We learned a lot during that panel that we used in our own group. And the nice part was that through Facebook and other media, we were able to stay connected despite the three-hour drive separating us. Now we're only thirty minutes apart; but, even with hectic schedules, it makes staying connected a real possibility.

WHAT HAS BEEN THE GREATEST BENEFIT OF YOUR PARTNERSHIP?

JAMIE: Aimie has become so much more than a critique partner. She's become a great friend. When you go through the ups and downs of the publishing industry together and trust each other with your most prized possessions (your works in progress), you can't help but become friends. We now celebrate milestones and birthdays together and take our kids on play dates (the play dates are for us). On the business side, Aimie is amazing about keeping me up-to-date on what's happening in the industry when I just want to bury my head in the sands of creativity. She keeps me balanced.

AIMIE: A savvy friend who knows the industry is invaluable. Jamie will tell you if those literary jeans make my butt look big (as in, maybe my query needs work or I need to tighten that first act) ... but she doesn't just dole out the negative. She gives me ideas on how to make it better. And having a true friend to celebrate your success is amazing. Jamie has been like my co-pilot in this crazy business, and I am thankful every day I have her in my life. There's a reason I dedicated a book to her.

What Has Been the Greatest Challenge of Your Partnership?

JAMIE: Time has become a mutual struggle since gaining a career in publishing. Because of deadlines, we often have to go through drafts so quickly that we don't get the opportunity to share them before sending it to our editors, or vice versa—a deadline might keep one of us from being available to read. It's a good problem to have! But I sometimes miss the days when we were more available to each other.

AIMIE: Time. Oh my goodness, time. We are both such driven, dedicated women that we have a hard time connecting long enough to support each other these days! And the demands of the publishing world make it next to impossible to get a beta read in before a manuscript is due. I am grateful when she and I do have the time to get together or share a passage from a WIP or discuss the industry. It's an amazing way to stay grounded and to reconnect with the craft.

What do you wish you would have known before you got started?

JAMIE: I think Aimie and I lucked out in finding each other because we fit really well as critique partners right off the bat and I have a feeling that doesn't happen very often. If someone is looking for a critique partner, I would encourage them to look for someone in their genre so they are both familiar with the "rules" of the genre. I would also make sure you're both clear on what kind of feedback each of you prefers to receive, that both of you are committed to giving feedback with kindness, and how often you want to share work. Make sure both of you are willing and able to support each other fairly and above all else—just like any relationship—communicate! Honest communication fills any holes that might appear as you begin to work together.

AIMIE: I was so clueless about how things were when I got into this business, I don't even know how to start that list. But one thing I know is that I should have been thanking Jamie every single day for creating an amazing critique group and for being my best friend and ally in the writing world.

HOW DOES YOUR PARTNERSHIP BETTER YOUR WRITING CRAFT?

JAMIE: What I love about Aimie and I is that we both have different strengths and weaknesses, which I believe is a huge benefit in a critique partner relationship. Aimie comes to me for emotional elements and romance, and I go to her for detail orientation and checking for consistency. I think it gives both of us more confidence in our work, knowing we have each other's backs.

AIMIE: The act of critiquing is huge. To see the faults in others' work is to see them in your own. And, of course, fresh eyes are invaluable in making an honest judgment of a piece. Jamie is my go-to when it comes to really making a scene come alive. She helps me to stop muddying the waters and to get to the real motivation behind what my characters want and what they're doing. I try to keep Jamie grounded in her own cannon. I'm a details person, and I help her to keep things tight. We're a great duo because we know what the other person needs.

What is your critique process?

JAMIE: At this point, we literally have no rules about how we critique for each other. Sometimes we ping each other for research questions; sometimes we send a sentence or paragraphs over Facebook Messenger to make sure something reads smoothly. And we are ALWAYS checking in with each other as we develop our characters or plots to get a second opinion. That's probably how we most often work with each other, and thankfully we live fairly close to each other so we get the opportunity to do this once every couple of months over coffee and Chinese food.

We don't get as much opportunity anymore to read each other's entire drafts, but we also have more confidence in our own abilities now, and we have editors to work with once we get to the point of having full drafts.

AIMIE: Nowadays, we work really on an ad hoc basis. At first, we never sent out so much as a query letter that the other person hadn't seen. We dissected entire manuscripts for each other all the time. Now, that level of involvement really isn't possible, but we still support each other as much as we can. For all of our successes, I do miss the good old days when we spent hours a day working together to reach the goal of becoming published authors. We made it, largely because of each other. I am so proud to have her as my friend and my critique partner.

About the Partners

JAMIE RAINTREE is the author of *Perfectly Undone* and *Midnight at the Wandering Vineyard*. She also teaches writers about business and productivity. Since the setting is always an important part of her books, she is happy to call the Rocky Mountains of Northern Colorado her home and inspiration.

Visit Jamie:

www.jamieraintree.com
www.facebook.com/jamieraintreeauthor
www.twitter.com/jamieraintree
www.instagram.com/jamieraintree/

AIMIE K. RUNYAN writes to celebrate history's unsung heroines. She is the author of two previous historical novels: *Promised to the Crown* and *Duty to the Crown*. She is active as an educator and a speaker in the writing community and beyond. She lives in Colorado with her wonderful husband and two (usually) adorable children.

Visit Aimie:

www.aimiekrunyan.com
www.twitter.com/aimiekrunyan
www.facebook.com/aimie.runyan.author

Kelsey Atkins, Tauri Cox, Devon Harry & Joy E. Rancatore

Focus Question: What unique challenges exist for your partnership of four writers, and how do you handle those challenges? What are the unique benefits to this group dynamic?

When we thought about this, we realized some of the benefits could also be challenges and vice versa. For instance, we have multiple partners to send our manuscripts to at different times. The challenge comes when we can't remember who has seen it at which stage of the revision process! With multiple partners, we get many different ideas and perspectives—which is great—but sometimes it can be idea overload. Processing all those thoughts can be overwhelming.

Another challenge unique to our situation is that we have more to critique and more storylines to keep up with; however, we also have the ability to say, "I can't right now." because usually at least one of us can help out. Always having someone available comes in handy when we're working on blurbs or trying to come up with character or place names or need some help figuring out an issue with a scene. We can send a quick tweet to the group and see who has some time. When we all participated in Camp NaNoWriMo (NaNo), we would do that with writing sprints. Sometimes two of us could work together; sometimes all of us could.

How did you meet?

We all met on Twitter through various chats and threads there, formed a behind-the-scenes messaging group with the purpose of bouncing ideas off one another and morphed into critique partners as our individual projects began to line up and we discovered we had similar goals for our writing. Participating in Camp NaNo together a few times solidified our writing relationships.

What has been the greatest benefit of your partnership?

KELSEY: It's helped me get out of my own head. With three different people to toss questions to, I can get quick feedback on a problem scene as I'm writing. With multiple critique partners, we also have more built-in cheerleaders, and it creates a bigger world for our writing. I can't imagine doing this without my critique partners.

TAURI: For me, it's gathering different perspectives. Some things may work for one CP and not for another. And if several CPs have issues with the same thing, then that's a major point to focus on! It's also nice that there's always someone at the same stage of writing as you. During Camp NaNo, Kelsey and Joy were both revising while Devon and I were working on first drafts. Each stage requires a different type of support and feedback; so, with four writers, you're always likely to have someone else in the same stage as you. I also think the emotional support is huge. Writing is often seen as a solitary activity, and it can be very isolating. Having a close friend to navigate the process alongside you is so meaningful.

DEVON: Having someone to bounce ideas off of and having other eyes on my work has helped me grow as a writer and helped me understand why things aren't working.

JOY: Partnering with multiple writers allows me greater objectivity and gives me the benefit of various perspectives for my work. Also, I get to watch their process. When I read multiple drafts of their works, I'm growing as well and learning things to improve my own revision process. It also shows me what they prefer and need from my critiques of their work, so I can give them better feedback in the future.

Because we're all different ages and in different stages of life and different parts of the U.S., we're also able to bring multiple opinions, worldviews, perspectives and more to the critiquing table.

WHAT HAS BEEN THE GREATEST CHALLENGE OF YOUR PARTNERSHIP?

KELSEY: My biggest challenge has been finding a balance to ensure I'm giving the right amount of time to each of my critique partners while still having time to focus on my own writing. I want to make sure I give each manuscript the attention it deserves but with four different books to critique, including my own, I often put my own work on the back burner.

TAURI: I agree that I think the time commitment can sometimes be a lot to handle. But the good thing is that there's no pressure with this group. If we have time, great. If not, there's no guilt. We all acknowledge that we have other things going on, so it's a nice balance.

DEVON: Because each of my partners may have read a different version of my manuscript, I can't always reach out to the group as a whole with a specific question. I can't ask the group's opinion on a character I added in the latest version that only one member has read so far. Another challenge is to listen to my gut even when my critique partners are calling for something different; I have to learn when to stand by what I know is true to my vision.

JOY: The biggest challenge for me has been learning how to properly evaluate the feedback I get from my critique partners and then determine if my reluctance to accept advice is due to my stubborn nature or to it genuinely being something I need to hold on to because it's vital to my vision and to my work. Through this, though, I've been able to learn more about who I am as a writer and about the purpose of my writing. I've also been able to think and react as a critic in order to defend or reject my reactions to the feedback.

WHAT DO YOU WISH YOU WOULD HAVE KNOWN BEFORE YOU GOT STARTED?

We came to a consensus that we really lucked out with our group because we mesh really well and work well together. We're all in similar places professionally and motivationally. The two primary things we mentioned wishing we would have known to ask were current and future genres and the time expectations.

How Does Your Partnership Better Your Writing Craft?

KELSEY: In all ways. Plot holes, writing block, and confusing scenes happen to the best of us. My scenes may make sense to me, but my critique partners can offer me a different perspective and show me what doesn't work.

TAURI: In my opinion, critique partners and beta readers are absolutely crucial. We are so close to our own projects, that it's often too hard to see the issues with a manuscript. A fresh and objective set of eyes is huge to the development process. And providing feedback to my CPs has also made me a better writer!

DEVON: Having qualified people to tell me what is and isn't working. Also, learning to critique my own work as I have more critique practice on others' work.

JOY: My critique partners have made me a better recipient of constructive criticism and a more empathetic writer. I consider many more aspects of my characters and scenes now than I did before I had the benefit of multiple points of view and perspectives on my writing.

What is a summary of your critique process?

We mostly prefer to hash out our "hot mess first drafts," do at least one round of our own revisions and then send that version out to the group. While we'll bounce ideas and brainstorm details and even send a line or two here and there during the first draft, we prefer to give a first polish before sending it out.

Individually, we are motivated, organized and driven with timelines to meet the goals we've set for ourselves and our writing. This helps us as a group to communicate our critiquing needs ahead of time. Since there are four of us, we have the ability to say no when our availability just doesn't line up with a need. That doesn't leave the writer in a bind because at least one of us should be available.

We have learned to communicate with one another about our expectations. We always ask what is expected for each critique, but we've also gotten to the point where we each have specific questions to send along with our manuscripts to guide the critique process.

For the most part, our critiques are given in separate documents with overall feedback to the manuscript as a whole and chapter-specific reactions. We do also make some comments in the body of the document when requested. These can vary from genuine reader reactions (that twist shocked me; I love this line; etc.) to highlighting confusing sentences or wordiness to light editing. Once again, we have learned to communicate our expectations ahead of time to make sure we're on the same page with what the writer needs on that version.

About the Partners

KELSEY ATKINS is an elementary and middle school teacher who loves to write. Her work with young adults in the classroom inspired her to write the *Finding the Light* series. Kelsey grew up in a small town in Idaho where she grew to love the outdoors. She currently lives in Boise, Idaho, with her husband and son. When she isn't teaching or writing, she enjoys spending time with her family, cooking, hiking, and volunteering at church.

Visit Kelsey:

www.findingthelightseries.com
www.twitter.com/AtkinsAuthor
www.instagram/AtkinsAuthor
www.facebook.com/findingthelightseries

Growing up, **TAURI COX** wanted to be a variety of things: marine biologist, veterinarian, equine chiropractor, neonatal surgeon. All biological, all scientific. Until she arrived at college and quickly discovered ... she was horrifically bad at science. But she also learned that she had a knack for  writing, and a passion was ignited. Since then, Tauri has graduated from the University of Texas where she studied creative writing and psychology under Elizabeth McCracken, five-time author and James A. Michener Chair in Fiction. Immediately afterward, she joined the Writer's Path at Southern Methodist University where she honed her skills. She now lives in Austin, TX, with her eighty-pound German Shepherd mix, her satanic cat, and a small shred of intact sanity.

Visit Tauri:

www.twitter.com/tauricox
www.facebook.com/tauricoxauthor/
www.instagram.com/tauricox/
www.tauricox.com

DEVON HARRY works a part-time job in retail and writes while at home. She currently has two finished novels and is in the querying process. She lives in Wisconsin with her boyfriend and big fat cat, Buffie. When she isn't writing, she's either watching Netflix, WWE Network or reading. You can visit her on all her social media sites!

Visit Devon:

www.authordevonharry.com
www.twitter.com/AuthorDevonH
www.instagram.com/authordevonharry/

Meet **JOY E. RANCATORE** in the About the Author section.

Appendix A: Collection of QWERTY Tips

- Search for answers to questions about your writing, its audience and purpose, through your own short fiction or nonfiction, blog articles or journaling. The beauty of exploration with shorter writing is you learn quickly because you achieve a completed piece faster. You can then revise, self-edit and further examine the piece in a timely manner to help you answer those introspective questions.
- Be respectful of your partner's circumstances or past and allow him to make the decision to either face sensitive topics in a manuscript or work around them. Don't make decisions for your critique partner. Allow him the dignity of choosing.

- Remember, a critique partner at the same level as you means you can more equally give to one another as you grow from and with each other.
- Notice any words or phrases your eyes hop over as you read and ask why they didn't hold your attention. Once you've answered that question a few dozen times, you will have a better grasp on good dialogue, and it will change the way you write spoken scenes.
- When you and your partner set out to learn your author voices, review multiple pieces you've written. Swap and review each other's pieces after you've examined your own. Work together to discover your natural ways of expression or *voice*. Studying already written pieces keeps you from conscious writing that forces an author voice instead of uncovering your natural one. Through this exercise, you'll learn your voice and your partner's. Plus, you will have accomplished an important task by working together.
- Throw in a little extra politeness when asking for a quick turnaround on a critique. Here's an example: "I know it's short notice, but I saw this contest today. I'd love to enter my article on boll weevils as polished as possible. Are you willing and able to provide an overall critique by November 12? Thanks for thinking on it!"

- Communication is key, regardless of the type of project under critique.
- Re-read your comments and commentary before sending them to your partner. Delete anything that attacks the person rather than the problem. If something lacks tact or compassion, erase and reword it.
- A well-constructed truth bomb commends the author's creativity or accomplishments, presents your opinion and leaves room for further discussion. Paired with specificity, this becomes a truth bomb that slays.

QWERTY Critique Truth Bomb Formula:
Commendation + Opinion + Discussion = Effective Truth x Specificity = Truth Bomb That Slays

- If you're having trouble connecting with a nonhuman character, remember all main and secondary characters—whether a toaster, robot, bear, flea or flying car—are personified characters with human characteristics. Find the emotional character arc, and you can then begin connecting with the hurting dragon robot, the talking car, the feeling flea.
- If you can't find anything word-wise to praise, look outside the page. Is it the author's first completed

piece? That's a big deal. Did this person fight tooth and nail to honor his designated writing time? That discipline is honorable, and you should commend him. Is the person's kind personality causing lack of conflict between characters? Praise the inherent characteristic, while reminding him that, like a person needs extra makeup during a photo shoot for the best results, stories require extra meanness toward the characters to spotlight story theme and overall purpose. Unfortunate events produce great stories.

BONUS QWERTY TIPS

We've prepared for you a few extra QWERTY Tips, specifically for critiquing your partner's narrative story:

- Think of each scene as a short story that requires a catchy beginning, a middle that doesn't lag, conflict relating to the setting and scene protagonist and an end that denotes change in the scene protagonist. This change doesn't have to be a huge, life-altering internal overhaul; but it should move the character toward the next point in his character arc. Also, it can sometimes link directly with the conflict in the scene. Without this key characteristic, the scenes will not stand the validity test, and you should remove or revise them. If the scene does have an emotional change for a character but it's repetitive and doesn't increase intensity from the last scene, remove the lesser scene, revise it to become valid or combine the twin scenes to hit your emotional bullseye.

- The opening chapter of the story is one of the most important in the lot. It has multiple important jobs; and, if it fails at any of them, a reader will most likely put your partner's book down. So, you need to know the basic functions of the opening chapter so you can identify imposters. The opening chapter should attract readers' attentions, introduce the main character and his initial problem, create a strong sense of setting and establish the mood and narrative voice of the entire book. Easy, right? (And all the authors laughed ... and then cried a little.)

- Track every character and subplot to make sure no loose ends exist at the project's conclusion. If you keep a notebook with the name of every character you come in contact with in the story and track their subplot with an arrow graph, you will be able to identify incomplete plot threads and unsatisfying character conclusions easily. You'll also be able to confidently articulate your thoughts regarding characters in relation to their subplot by referencing the graph.

- The story's resolution needs to provide closure. It's more than making sure all of your plot threads have nice knots at the end of them. Resolutions should leave the reader with a pleasant or unpleasant contentment or a lingering wonder of the story's characters in a fashion consistent with genre expectations. You'll make this evaluation based solely on how you feel. Because of this, it may be hard to articulate to your partner. One way to add objectivity is to make sure the character's arc and resolution fit together or note if the character is acting outside of his personality. Also, if you know you prefer a happy ending and your partner's book is not providing that, be sure to step back from your personal opinions to determine if the character's resolution has been brought about logically based upon the obstacles he had to overcome. If that's true, then your preference doesn't matter in this case.
- When you look at the plot as a whole and try to break it down with logic bombs and reason grenades, will it survive? This may be a good time to write down your concerns regarding the plot points and talk it out with your CP. You won't have a productive discussion, however, if you haven't taken a quiet moment to consider potential issues.

Appendix B: Strengths & Weaknesses Challenge

ARE YOU STILL UNSURE how to develop your magic strengths and weaknesses list? That's okay! We will take the process one step at a time in this Challenge.

Step 1: Take between three and five pieces you've written and note where you're proud and where you would like to improve. False modesty or inflated ego have no place in this exercise. In order for this to work and for you to grow, you must be level-headed and unbiased. We believe this process works best when you haven't looked at the piece in at least a week. Evaluating more than one piece helps you pinpoint patterns in your writing and gives you tangible proof of your abilities. Solidify your list of strengths with specific details you believe you did well. Likewise, make your list of weaknesses based on proof of the areas you would like to improve. We have the tendency to be mean to ourselves, often unnecessarily. Providing proof either way will help you stay honest to yourself and enable you to produce an accurate list.

Step 2: Take several pieces you didn't write but admire. Write down why you love them and what brings you back to them. Is it the words, the characters, the descriptions, the dialogue, the pacing? Be specific and include excerpts from the text for you to return to in the future. Evaluate if you are implementing some of these things you appreciate in your own writing. These can go under your strengths column if you feel proud of your application. Next, pinpoint the things you'd like to do but are unsure how to or have tried unsuccessfully. Those go under the challenge or weakness column. Now we have goals to reach. We QWERTYs love a good goal!

Step 3: If you've had feedback on anything you've written, now is the time to compile it. These aspects belong on your lists as well if you find supporting proof in your work. If you've had unsubstantiated negative feedback—not solid constructive criticism—weigh it against the evaluations you've done for yourself. If it doesn't add up and you can't find textual proof of their opinions, you know you can logically discount those thoughtless words, leaving them behind as you step toward your writing future.

Through this three-step process, you might discover something you thought was a strength is not. Maybe you think you're a master at dialogue, but you're repeatedly given dialogue pointers. Perhaps you should revisit your dialogue with an open mind and willingness to improve if needed. Likewise, a perceived weakness may be a strength at this point, thanks to your focused attention. You have a strength you can now use to assist another writer. How exciting is that?

All legitimate suggestions can aid you in finalizing your list of strengths and weaknesses. Take a moment to celebrate how far you've already come! Now you're ready to move forward with a game plan of what you know and what you need help improving in your writing.

Appendix C: Critique Partner Interview Questionnaire

THIS COMPREHENSIVE INTERVIEW SHEET is for you and any potential CPs to fill out. Use it as is, add to it or simply let it be a template for your own. This interview can be helpful at any stage. If you're in an established partnership, try it out with your current CP, whether you've been together a month or ten years. You will learn more about one another and perhaps strengthen your partnership.

The interview is split in two parts: professional and personal. If you're using this to vet potential partners, we recommend you complete the professional part first, take time to evaluate it and decide if this person might be a good writer fit before you move into the deeper personal questions.

PROFESSIONAL INFORMATION

CRAFT KNOWLEDGE AND NEEDS

Share the Strengths & Weaknesses Challenge with your potential CP if he is not currently reading *Finders Keepers*.

- What are your strengths regarding the writing craft?
- What are your weaknesses regarding the writing craft?
- What genres do you prefer to write?
- What type of writing do you do (e.g., short fiction, nonfiction essays, fiction or creative nonfiction novels, historical flash fiction, poetry)?
- What project are you working on now?

GOALS

- Are you writing for a career, for personal fulfillment or both?
- What do you want to do with your writing after you consider it done?
- What are your aspirations as an author?
- How many pieces do you plan to need critiqued each year? Do you expect more than one critique on each piece? If so, please estimate how many critiques total you expect and share the length for each project (novel, novella, short story, etc.).

- How do you think this partnership will benefit your goals?

CRITIQUE PREFERENCES

Consider sharing the Critique Structure Questionnaire with your potential CP to help them with this section.

- Do you have any writing style restrictions, something you will not critique because of personal aversion (e.g., particular points of view, multimedia books, certain tropes)?
- Are you willing to critique other genres outside of the one you write?
- What kind of critique do you generally give when you evaluate original work …?
    - I present the comment with an analogy or example if it's possible to ease the author into the suggestion and see my thought process. I also indicate where I believe things have gone right.
    - I state what I think is good and bad with blunt simplicity and little emotion.
    - I state my suggestions in a way that also shows my personal emotions.
    - I point out what's wrong with the piece and my personal reactions of the author. If I don't say anything about a section, he should assume it's fine.

- How do you approach deadlines? Do you regularly set and meet these for your writing?
- Are you able to give 100 percent to a critique, even if it's not in your preferred genre or style, and meet the deadline agreed upon by you and your partner once you accept to fill this need of your critique partner?

Disclaimer for the last question: *Everyone has been through something. Share only what you are comfortable with. You do not owe me nor do I owe you any exposition regarding these topics.*

- Are there topics or content that, due to personal experiences or religious convictions, you are currently unwilling to read about and critique in a piece because it will compromise your mental or spiritual health? (e.g., a particular type of abuse, graphic physical experiences, gruesome horror, demonic activities, bullying, roller coasters, drowning or other triggers)

PERSONAL INFORMATION

ENTERTAINMENT PREFERENCES

- What genres do you prefer to read?
- What are your top five favorite books you've ever read?

- What are you currently reading or what was the last book you read?
- Is there a book you hate? If so, why?
- Are you willing to read other types and genres of writing?
- What genres will you NOT read?
- Outside of writing, what hobbies do you enjoy?
- Do you have some favorite TV shows or movies? If so, what are they?

Past Or Current Situations

- What is your professional background?
- What is your job situation and what time availability or restrictions do you have for critiquing?
- How long have you been writing?
- What led you to writing as a creative pursuit?

Your Approach To Writing

- What is your primary purpose in writing? Why do you have to write?
- Would you consider yourself goal-oriented or more free-spirited in regards to your writing?
- Are there any details about your personal worldview (e.g., religious affiliation, political leanings, etc.) you feel are important for me to understand or that might affect your critiques?

Appendix D: Critique Structure Questionnaire

THESE QUESTIONS ARE SPECIFIC to the piece you're now asking your partner to review. You know each other now; you've talked about how you need your critiques to be presented. Now it's time to get down to the nitty-gritty. If you answer the following questions before each critique, you should receive the most beneficial feedback and may avoid many frustrating misunderstandings.

- **What are your goals for my involvement with this work in progress?** This includes the type of critique needed, the number of read-throughs expected and the future details like marketing blurbs, query letters and advertisement copy. Think through what might be needed and decide how the critiquing partner can

best help. This list will be revised through discussion, and you will suddenly have a plan.
- **What is my deadline for this critique?** Set up a deadline with a standard week buffer. If something unforeseen happens to delay a critique, communicate that immediately with a new plan in place for fulfillment of the commitment. If there's no time to add a cushion, make sure both of you are on board with the tight timeline.
- **What are your compensation expectations for this critique?** When you answer this with the expectation of a reciprocal critique, you may be able to put your partner's critiquing dates on your calendar in the same conversation.
- **Remind me of your critiquing presentation needs as discussed during our Interview Questionnaire (e.g., gentle comments or blunt observations, hold the niceties).** This review helps each of you remember about needs like a separate letter style with all the big picture details instead of a response at the end of each chapter or comments throughout. It also reminds you about requests for weekly email updates or text messages of favorite quotes.
- **How should I get my critique information back to you?** We're thinking specifically about document formats: Word, PDF, RTF, Pages, etc. Remember, if the critiquing partner needs to type directly on the

file, whichever form is chosen should be compatible with the person's computer and technology. Also, you need to be honest about your abilities. If you don't know how to use the "track changes" feature, tell your partner. He may give you a tutorial.

- **After your critique, how and when should we communicate?** Would you rather have a phone call or video chat or an email? Decide on the communication avenue and put a date (or dates) on the calendar.
- **What is your genre and theme for this piece?** The critiquing partner needs to apply tropes, structure and other genre knowledge to the critique. If what the author presents doesn't match what the partner discovers, you can discuss why it doesn't work.
- **Please provide me with specific questions or concerns you're struggling with in this piece.** If you're giving the critique, you should read these questions carefully before you begin, ask clarifying questions if necessary and refer back to them to be sure you're focusing on the right details as you critique.
- **What are your publishing goals for this project?** The answer to this question will most likely drive some of the big picture changes to a manuscript.

Appendix E: Surviving Writing Critique Groups

WHILE THIS BOOK FOCUSES on the dynamic partner relationship two (or a small handful of) writers can have with one another, chances are you have been—or will be—involved in a critique group dynamic. Because we recognize these situations present specific challenges, we decided they deserve a few dedicated words.

BENEFITS OF CRITIQUE GROUPS

The QWERTY ideal for a critique group includes an attentive leader and ten or fewer equally committed writers who meet often—weekly, if possible—to brainstorm, support and encourage while critiquing from researched knowledge with kindness and respect. A situation like this can be as advantageous as having multiple critique partners, as expressed in *Finders Keepers*.

One benefit of a critique group is you will get varying opinions and different feedback in one take. You will need to sort through and compare them to your project standards. However, in this type of situation, the advice you get will be well-founded and transferable to other projects.

You'll also benefit from hearing how other projects are evaluated and how other authors are critiqued. An indirect benefit comes by experiencing critique styles that either encourage or dishearten. You'll see firsthand how others respond to varying critique styles. Even if some advice doesn't resonate with you, you will witness how each personality requires an individualized critique strategy.

Questions and brainstorming are critique group strong points. You'll get multiple immediate answers that can help you move forward in your current project. Also, ideas will be tossed back and forth as you explore a topic. You may not use any of them, but your right brain will feed off all the creative energy and could produce story answers you've been needing.

Each member of the group comes with unique experiences and knowledge, along with a variety of worldviews and personal reactions. Members can give you advice you never would have considered and opportunities to learn more about craft and critique than you would have alone. They may also impart a broader sense of who your future readers are and how you might market to them. Each member will be studying and consuming craft-related information between meetings, so your group could be a writing think tank, boosting your knowledge exponentially. Plus, they could become a built-in support team as you head toward submission or publication.

The problem is, they're so easy to get wrong.

Types of Critique Groups and Their Challenges

ACADEMIC GROUPS

If you dedicated time to writing in high school or as part of your collegiate field of study, you may have been introduced to critique groups in an academic setting. Since a grade is at stake and the teacher should be a careful moderator of the situation, you should—in theory, anyway—receive criticism that is founded on writing craft knowledge and directed toward the work, not the author's abilities or lack thereof.

To make critiquing a fully beneficial experience in a classroom setting, the instructor should spend adequate time explaining the process and its purpose. Guiding questions can aid in this endeavor and close moderation is vital to keep students' focus on the work rather than the writers behind it. A class full of invested students who care about you and the craft, equal to their need for a great grade, could teach you exponentially more than traditional classes might.

However, you may find your academic peers don't provide much helpful feedback. Their investment in your work might only be as deep as their desire for a passing grade, which leads to apathy concerning your personal growth and a half-hearted critique.

Often this setting requires cold readings, where the students bring in copies of their work for everyone, someone reads it out loud and then the critiquing commences. This type of critique does not naturally allow for in-depth reflection, but it's an excellent way to gauge honest reader reactions.

Even when distribution of the piece ahead of time is required, students may or may not have read it. While this is a negative consequence to mandatory critique groups, discoveries exist in all life situations—even if it's just learning what behaviors you should steer clear of or experiencing criticism and evaluation of your work by others, even if it's only two or three.

Just remember: if you are a part of a struggling academic critique group, it will be over at the end of the semester. At that point, you can seek out a critique group or partner of your choosing.

COMMUNITY WRITING GROUPS

Your hometown has a writers' critique group, and you want to join. This is wonderful! Go visit and learn how this group ticks. Some of the same challenges from the last section apply in this new setting, though these types of groups are generally well-organized and have caring members. The groups that thrive hand out pieces for critique far enough in advance to encourage members to read and reflect before sharing in public.

These groups also face challenges by the wide range of writing purposes, craft knowledge and experience levels of each member. If a group is comprised of hobby writers, aspiring authors and seasoned published authors, each member must understand the varying needs and work harder to respect one another. Likewise, such a fellowship possibly includes diversity in genres. Each member should respect writing different from theirs and embrace the study required to understand each genre's specifications.

Another issue comes with time. Like any commitment in life, this one must be weighed carefully. Do you have the time you need to consistently and thoroughly critique all the work submitted? The length of time needed changes with the group size, so you must be honest with yourself and the other members if this isn't an attainable commitment for you right now. People are counting on your honesty, just as you are counting on theirs.

The danger in a group setting—once again depending on size and setup—is the potential for the loss of recognition of an author's voice and style. In a carefully crafted critique partnership, each writer gets to know the other's voice. While this ability only takes a critique or two in the relationship we've examined through this book, it could take much longer—if it happens at all—within the context of a larger setting where you may have any number of voices and styles to learn.

While academic critiquing typically focuses on short, assigned work, critique groups of this nature more often include longer pieces, often book length. Unless this group is committed to reading full manuscripts for every member, you're only getting a peephole glimpse into another's mansion. This cripples your ability to critique for big picture issues.

Critiquing, as we've discussed, should focus on overall issues or specific author questions. However, when you don't have the full piece, the advice you give and receive may be based on assumption rather than truth, or you may find yourself focusing on the smaller details—like misplaced commas or misused words—that belong in the much later stage of editing. This could result in unhelpful advice altogether or a novel with perfect comma placement and a giant sinkhole in its plot.

Just as you wouldn't analyze the architecture of a mansion based on a distorted view of the front hallway, writers may want to reconsider providing a critique of a novel based on a mere 500 words.

Critique Group Situations That Don't Work

We see great danger in poorly moderated situations or groups where members' motivations are self-centered. Any group where members do not have basic respect for the people around them is destined to break spirits. A critique group should follow all the same leading principles fleshed out through this book, including communication, honesty, respect and a mutual desire to grow and learn together.

Often, especially in the case of an academic setting, you may be stuck in an unhelpful or even abusive situation. We urge you to speak to your teacher, professor or group leader. Take your concerns to a higher administrator when the classroom manager is part of the problem. Such an extreme case does not allow for learning, and the only education likely to arise from such a situation is a degree in distrust of fellow humans.

If you are in a group critique situation that is bad for you and it's something you can walk away from, do it. Plain and simple. Even if you desire advice and an opportunity to grow, you may struggle with the face-to-face, in-the-moment feedback or the fact that all this takes place in front of an audience. You shouldn't remain in a situation that's damaging to your mental and emotional health. Perhaps having a critique partner would be a better dynamic for you. You may also consider starting your own critique group and fostering an atmosphere fitting to you and other like-minded writers.

If you cannot walk away and it's not an extreme situation, seize this as an opportunity. Put the experience into perspective and use it to see what *not* to do and how to better your critiquing techniques. Also, be sure you're open to accepting appropriate criticism. Constructive advice helps you grow, but it cannot do that if you automatically shut down and refuse to accept anything less than shining praise for your work. Even the greatest writers in the world can learn something new.

How to Critique in a Group Setting

If you are in a critique group or plan to be, we'd like to give you a few practical tips to make your experience as beneficial as possible.

Stick to the Weather.

When your group meets once a month or less and you find yourself surrounded by writers of every level of experience with diverse goals, it's unlikely you will really *know* the people around you. Especially when you're new to the group, you may not know the hobby writer from the professional. The issue with this is, you should—ideally—critique those two writers differently. The hobbyist most likely wants a few simple tips but mostly encouragement. The career writer needs tough love and careful critiquing in order to excel in his chosen profession.

If you're unsure of each writer's needs, we recommend you steer clear of religion-and-politics topics and stick to the weather, until you know what each author needs. As in conversations with people you don't know well, your critique of an acquaintance shouldn't dive to the depths of a controversial or deep issue, nor should you respond belligerently when they turn out to have conflicting opinions. For example, you may want to correct the campy dialogue and deviation from genre norms regarding a piece the author shared, but we caution you to wait. Until you know the author's background, stick to the weather. The author you're about to unknowingly shatter with a critique he's not emotionally ready for has just taken his first brave steps toward getting his work out there. He should be encouraged to write and share more. Let him get to his feet and then help him walk.

Start with smaller details—perhaps stick to offering some leading questions about the character's motivations or the writer's choice of setting—and stack encouraging words alongside them. As you get to know the writers better, you can tailor your critiques to each one's actual needs.

If you're only getting a few thousand words of larger manuscripts here and there, without any discussion of the bigger picture, you may find it impossible to give an actual critique and need to stick with obvious issues like grammar, syntax and scene basics instead. As you continue with a group, you may find ways to offer further critique in one-on-one opportunities as you pick out the writers who have similar goals to you. You will also begin to read body language and recognize when a writer wants more. Once you're comfortable with that and recognize where you can offer more detailed critiquing assistance, go for it!

SAY WHAT YOU KNOW.

If you haven't turned a weakness into a strength yet, group settings are not the time to practice. For example, you shouldn't attempt a complete dialogue critique in public when you are still learning the art of dialogue. However, if you have been reading a book about it or stumbled upon a couple of articles you bookmarked to study, sharing those resources is perfectly acceptable.

If you have a firm grasp on pacing and confidence that you can articulate advice on the matter, that's what you focus on in your critique. Very few writers can be a master of everything; but every writer has his strengths. Hone yours and then share them. People in your group will seek you out for your expertise and appreciate you for it.

Utilize Questions More Than Statements.

Questions are a critique's magic weapons. They help you help the writer and his piece without accidently providing ill-suited or offensive advice. Because you're only getting a tiny piece of the larger manuscript, you may feel strongly about a suggestion but later find that it actually breaks the piece instead of repairing it.

If you can get the author's mental wheels turning by asking him a good question, he will provide a fitting answer. If anything, perhaps the writer's answer will enable you to provide more relevant advice; or it may raise another question for him to consider, while bringing him closer to self-discovery.

BE AWARE OF TENSION OR ANXIETY IN THE ROOM.

You're likely to have a group member who hasn't read this article and who is oblivious to differing writer needs around him. He won't notice when he's been camped out on a religion topic for too long. He won't care that the author before him is beet-red and ready to slide under the foundation of the building. In an ideal group, you'll have a moderator who guides the conversations in such a way that you don't reach such an extreme situation; however, if you don't, perhaps you can be that person.

If you're unable to intervene, you may be able to comfort and reassure the writer afterward or kindly but firmly call out the person doing the extreme critiquing.

If you're giving a critique, be aware of the writer's body language. Test when you can go deeper but know the signs of when you've gone as far as you should.

BE CONCISE.

The most important thing in a group situation is to be concise. Part of the value of a critique group is the opportunity to hear from every member. That can't happen if we don't monitor the time we take to give our critiques.

The first way to maintain brevity is to know your point before you speak. Let's say you're first in order to offer feedback. It's okay to say, "I need a few minutes to get my thoughts together. Can you come back to me?" Jot down key words or points to share so, when you get the chance, you can toss them out quickly.

Listen to other members to make sure you don't repeat them or to note if you have something to add. If others have shared what you were thinking about the piece before it's your turn, don't repeat it. Say something new or don't say anything at all.

Remember a specific example, if called for, to illustrate your point. You should use one from the piece shared in the group, but examples from your own writing or from well-known works can also get a point across. The danger with this lies in wordiness. If you spend fifteen minutes giving a synopsis of a movie before you finally get to the one little nugget that can help the writer, you've likely taken your time and someone else's. If you find yourself rambling, end your critique, gather your thoughts and approach the author after the meeting.

SHARE RESOURCES.

Finally, it might be that the best you can offer is to point the writer in the correct direction for further study. If you have resources on a topic that could improve the author's piece, ask if you can share.

How to Handle Stereotypical Group Members

Stereotypes exist for a reason. In a group setting, you're likely to have one or more of the following characters, so we came up with some ways to coexist when necessary.

ONE-UPPER

You know that guy, right? The one who knows just a little more than everyone else. The one who's played poker with Stephen King and has the keys to the plotting kingdom. Honestly, the best thing you can do is ignore him. He's mostly harmless, and it won't kill you to hear his "I had a heart-to-heart chat with James Patterson" story for a hundredth time.

KNOW-IT-ALL/BAD ADVICE GIVER

This guy is the bullying cousin of the One-Upper. He'll tell you all the hard-and-fast rules of writing, according to him. We know better, right? Writing has very few no-exception rules. Besides, rules were made to be broken—with understanding of craft, of course. He may even pass off incorrect information as gospel truth, and trying to interrupt him to set the record straight can be harder than opening a rusted can lid with a toothpick. We know this guy's an inevitable part of life sometimes, so how do we deal with him? If he's jumping up and down on your manuscript like a kid on a bouncy castle, don't play his game. Be a duck. Let his ill-founded words roll off your back and keep on swimming.

The leader of your group should be moderating the situation. If he's not, though, try to change the topic. If that doesn't work and you're an observer of his childishness, consider going after the meeting to the author facing the know-it-all's trampling and give encouragement and correction to the misinformation. If well-received, add some kind, constructive criticism for that writer. Depending on the situation, you could counteract the negative or incorrect advice by stating what you think and adding, "It all depends on style."

Joy witnessed a perfect example of that phrase's power in a critique group. The discussion turned toward dialogue. One member asked for advice and shared her thoughts. Several other members launched directly into a litany of "you-have-tos." Finally, after a few rounds of overlapping and contradicting advice, another member interjected with a much-needed voice of reason. He used the "it-all-depends-on-style" line and backed it with a reputable source. That ended the dialogue on dialogue that day ... and hopefully the misinformation about it.

Mr. Better Than You

This person leaves an ooze of "better-than" in his wake. He's likely to take jabs at the writer, rather than discovering both value and need for the piece and focusing on the writer's growth. Better Than Yous are the bullies whose advice you never listen to. It's rare we speak in absolutes, so take note.

The Stirrer-Upper

This is the person who's always got a controversial story to tell about another group member or has something to complain about. He will pit one member against the other to cause dissension in the group. Steer clear of him to keep from falling into his trap of lies or fanning the flames of his discontent. Surround yourself with positive people and exude positivity yourself by looking for ways to build up the group and its members.

Writing critique groups can be beneficial—remember the Inklings?—however, not every one is set up for success and not every writer is cut out for this specific dynamic. Be honest with yourself and observant within your critique group. Hopefully, this article will help you decide if your involvement holds value for your author life.

Appendix F: Mea's Theory of Fear

First explained on QWERTY Writing Life Podcast, Season 1, Episode 5. Transcript adapted to prose for your reading convenience.

Disclaimer: *This theory is the process by which I overcome fear on a daily basis, and I hope it helps someone who is a fearful creature, like me. If it is not academically sound, however, I don't want to know. Just because I'm sharing it with you, doesn't mean you have to implement it in your life. Let's just agree to disagree and talk about stories instead. Thanks!*

~ Mea

FEAR. It's such a tiny, harmless-looking word. I mean, it only has four letters and takes up half an inch or so on this page. But, if we're adding length based on the intensity of the emotion, with the way it takes over our lives, it should be three million miles long.

Fear is one of the reasons humans are still around, though; so let's review it as a help rather than an obstacle for a moment.

Human A sees a wild bear in the woods. We'll call this human Jim. Jim wants to pet the animal's furry head—an action that is outside of his normal routine, but that bear is so darn cute. Fear points out the bear's sharp claws and the baby cub behind him. It suggests running away instead, since the bear is now showing Jim his teeth. Jim heeds the advice and doesn't approach the bear. Jim lives another day.

Human B is visiting Ireland. Her name is Cody. It's Cody's first time away from her landlocked hometown. Cody wants to walk the edge of the Cliffs of Moher but, on the way there, is pushed to her knees by the wind. Fear dulls the shiny idea of role-playing a part from a BBC literary classic—it's much safer away from the craggy edge—and Cody returns to her hometown intact.

Human C—Ken—finds a beautiful berry growing from a fence row. It smells sweet, and his mouth waters in anticipation of the taste. An image of Ken's neighbor suffering from food poisoning last year causes his stomach to ache in empathy, and the fear of clutching a toilet for the better part of a week (or worse) makes him throw the lovely fruit into the pasture.

Thank you, Fear, for your service. Kindly accept this fist bump.

Fear protects us by trying to stop us from doing *anything* that takes us outside our comfort zone. It's not our enemy. It's not trying to hurt us. It's supposed to keep us alive, and it will. We will not die if we stay as we are.

[In most comfort zone cases. However, if you are in a domestic violence or emotional abuse situation, please seek help. You deserve it. Call 800-779-7233.]

Our "comfort zones" are not always comfortable, though. Say you're in a job that you don't like, but it pays the bills. Fear reminds you you're fed, you're not broke and you sleep under a roof. "You're winning!" it praises.

Then, one day, you start thinking, What if I just looked at the job postings at another place. Maybe update my resume. Surely, life has got to be better than this.

Fear's alert hits critical. "Hold on, Hoss," it says. "Didn't you just hear me say, 'Winning!'?"

Why did this happen? Because fear is a natural response when we consider change. You shouldn't be shocked at the appearance of fear. You should expect it, actually.

Fear doesn't have discernment. It can't tell the difference between types of change, just the intensity of it. A change that may threaten your basic needs (physical safety, food, water) produces the same kind of fear as a change to your self-esteem (psychological, self-fulfillment needs), for example. According to Maslow's Hierarchy of Needs, once your basic needs are fulfilled, you become concerned with other, higher levels, such as your self-esteem. But, fear thinks every hint of change is going to displace you from your basic needs. If you really want to be a writer, fear sees that as a big threat to the status quo it understands as your comfort zone and to your survival. Fear sounds a little melodramatic, but remember, it has what it believes to be our best interests at heart.

After years of allowing fear to control my decisions, here's what I've determined: fear is my fiercely loyal, oversized imaginary pet dog. It growls at everything that could potentially cause me danger. I evaluate the situation and, if I find the situation truly dangerous, I let go of his leash and allow the good boy to protect me. But, if my evaluation finds that the change approaching is an acquaintance whom I'd like to befriend, I pet Fear's head, whisper comforting words and keep his leash firm in my hand.

Fear is the consequence of change. We humans don't do change well; so, at even the notion of change, our instinct will do anything to keep us in status quo, like allowing fear to spread unwarranted, until it consumes our thoughts and paralyzes our actions, a mental epidemic.

Fear shouldn't be a deterrent to achieve your goals or desires. It should, however, be a trigger to stop and evaluate what you're actually afraid of and ask the question, "Is this decision worth changing your life?"

Don't let fear be an excuse that holds you back from becoming who you want to be.

The first line of defense against allowing fear to consume you is to hold it up against an image of who you are now and an image of who you want to be. Which of those options is fear protecting? Is it the right one? If so, press onward. If not, pet Fear on the head, tug on his leash a little if you must, but continue on. You have things to do.

Finally, since fear is awakened by change and if creating something is your goal, make the act of creating a part of your normal so fear can learn to accept it.

Now, go make something.

Appendix G: Joy's Time Tips

IF YOU COULD HAVE more of any one thing, what would it be? I'm going to guess most of you answered, "Time!" I agree. Do you know what I've discovered? We can maximize time ... and even create more of it.

Before you all start throwing hundreds my way—though I wouldn't say no to a few of those—I don't mean *literally* increasing the hours in a day. You can create more time by better utilizing the twenty-four hours you've got, and I've got ten literal ways for you to do just that!

1. Get organized.

This will look different for everyone, but I can share my top three organizational steps.

ORGANIZE EMAIL FOLDERS.

I create email folders for all the messages I either can't read right away, want to reference later or want to respond to when I can. I also have a folder for inspirational emails—kind words from readers.

ORGANIZE WORK SPACES.

When I tidy up my desk area and make it as free of clutter as possible, I'm instantly more productive. This isn't always achievable for me since my "office" is a shared space, plus it's also our dining room/living room/school room.

ORGANIZE YOUR CALENDAR.

I set up a scheduling system I can access whenever, regardless of where I am. I have tried to keep electronic calendars, but it simply does not work for me. Pen and paper is a must. I found the perfect printable planner made with writers in mind, so now I carry my little planner in a binder around the house with me, keep it on my nightstand at night and toss it in my purse or bag whenever I go somewhere. I totally stole the idea from Mea! Now, in addition to having my calendar in my binder, I also have sections for each work in progress, for blog posts, for social media ideas, for writing craft notes, for story ideas, for project planning and for conference notes. I love having all that stuff in one spot!

2. Know YOU.

In order to both simplify and maximize time, you must know your ultimate goals and what is most important in your life. Take some time alone to reflect and jot down what these are for you. Keep them handy and reference them often. This grounded focus keeps me zeroed in on where my time should be spent.

3. Plan ahead.

Think through all the tasks that fill your time. How can you plan ahead to accomplish some of these?

For example, earlier this week I thought through my social media posting and jotted out a three-month plan. I went ahead and scheduled the remainder of that first month and planned when to schedule the rest. An hour or two a month will save me an hour or two every week. Sure, some posts can't be scheduled; and I will still interact with my followers, but I'm not trying to formulate a post last-minute, so my content is better quality. Plus, I won't forget to post—or have posting foiled by a bout of flu and bronchitis.

Consistency is key in building a faithful following, and planning bolsters consistency.

I'm working toward spending only four full afternoons a month on writing my blog posts. I can write two posts one day, two posts another day and then type up, format and edit them over one or two more days. That will save me a great deal of time and help when life gets crazy and changes in my schedule happen. Plus, I should be able to produce better quality posts when I write ahead. Even if my idea is a good one, slapping it all together on the day before posting is *not* the way to write a quality post.

The steps I've taken toward achieving this goal include polling followers to learn what posts they like. From there, I've implemented a topic for each week of the month. Now that I know the broad topics, I can sit down a month ahead, work out a focus and write them.

In my home life, meal planning makes a *huge* difference for time and finances. When I fall out of my meal planning habits, it impacts my productivity. Instead, if I sit down and plan out our meals a week, two weeks or—best of all—a month at a time, I save an incredible amount of time. Also, because I'm planning ahead for a longer time period, I save money by choosing meals with similar ingredients. I can buy a big bag of potatoes to spread out over the month. I know they'll get used and won't go to waste, and I'm buying one item instead of five. Fewer trips to the store equals fewer impulse buys and splurges. Better yet, I place the order on my phone, schedule a pickup, pull up and have them place the groceries in my trunk. Take that, checkout line temptations and clearance clothes!

4. Set times.

Every successful person I know does this—time blocking, "batching," scheduling. Regardless of what you call it, planning specific days and times for specific work is a must and will maximize time. Basically, you look at your calendar and plan blocks of time to devote to various tasks, jobs or writing projects.

Every weekday, I block off 8:00 a.m. to noon. This is when I homeschool my children. We complete all of our work together during this time. If they are productive and focused that morning, they will also be able to complete, turn in and receive their independent work back with a grade before lunch.

Now, one of my children is an early bird who loves mornings. He wakes up early, gets to work on his assignments for the day and stays focused throughout the morning 99 percent of the time. He's typically done before noon. Like he says, "The quicker I get my work done, the quicker I get to play and do other stuff!" My other child? Well, let's just say she leans more to the procrastinating side of things. She takes twenty minutes to settle into a worksheet, does a problem and looks around for ten more minutes and … well, you get the picture, right? She throws my time blocks in disarray; however, she knows that I will complete my teaching with her and she'll work all day if she has to, but I have to get to work after lunch.

Noon to 1:00 p.m. I should be preparing and feeding my kids their lunch and doing household chores. My set daily work time is 1:00 p.m. to 3:00 p.m. Then I fill in the rest of my time blocks with specific responsibilities: writing, cooking dinner, preparing Sunday school lessons, prepping school lessons, marketing my books and preparing for speaking engagements or our QWERTY podcast. Everything I do has a block of time. Every block of time gets specific to dos each day/week. On the day I originally typed this post, I set aside my 1-to-3 block for typing up, formatting and editing two blog posts and adding on the computer all the revisions I made to a short story.

When you schedule your time and specify what you'll be doing, focus comes easier; and better focus helps further maximize time. When you know you've got exactly thirty minutes to write a post, you settle in to the zone and make it happen. With an open-ended chunk of time and no deadlines … forget about it!

Flexibility is another good thing about time blocks. I don't know about you, but my days are anything but normal and predictable. My husband has a job where his schedule changes every day. Sometimes he opens;

sometimes he's a mid; other times he closes. Usually he has all three of those shifts throughout the course of a week, and each shift changes when I set my writing times. His day or two days off aren't always the same days of the week, and his schedule could change at the last minute.

So, I need flexibility! With my time blocks, I can pick up a block and mentally move it around as needed. I know what things I can skip when necessary. When his schedule permits, my husband does many of the household tasks, which allows me to focus elsewhere. Every now and then, my kids get in an ambitious, helpful mood; and they'll actually follow the list of daily household chores I have posted. When they pitch in and take those off my plate, I can fill those time blocks with something else.

5. Use timers.

Closely following #4, you *have* to stick to the times you set. For example, if I'm going to make my 3:00 to 4:00 p.m. time block for reading to my kids, I have to finish my work at 3:00. The challenge I have is, when I start to work or write, I get in a zone and will keep going. Unfortunately, I *can't* just keep going. My days stay full of many different responsibilities, so I have to help myself stay within my blocks. That's where timers come in to play.

6. Communicate plans.

This one rounds out the last two steps. You cannot hope to have effective time blocks if you don't share them with your family. If I don't let my kids know that we'll read for an hour if they give me two hours of undisturbed work time after lunch, they're going to try my patience the entire time. I won't finish my work, and they'll be upset when we don't read.

If my husband doesn't know I have a tight editing deadline and need all the time I can get to meet it, he won't know I need extra help around the house or that he may only see the back of my head for a while.

7. Choose *right*.

We have countless ways we could spend our time. Many of them—even most of them—are great things. Podcasts, courses, webinars, articles, blog posts, Twitter chats, videos, conferences, etc. All great—so many free and available constantly at our fingertips.

The thing is, with all the great stuff surrounding us, we have to choose what's *right* for us. For example, I may only have time for listening to two podcasts, so I need to quickly scroll through all the *great* and find the *right* two for me.

8. Cut extras.

Think through all of your activities and responsibilities and make a list. Now compare this list to the one full of goals and most important things from #2. If something on this list doesn't aid in achieving one of those goals or isn't something you are most passionate about, cut it out of your life. This can sometimes be difficult, but it has to be done so you can simplify and maximize your time.

9. Be ready.

Keep a notepad on hand for whenever inspiration strikes. Make sure your planner's always nearby so you can reference it often to jog your memory on the tasks you've scheduled. Keep whatever tools you need for your work time in their proper place, ready to go when you are.

I have a morning routine that sets me up for success when I follow it. To stick to that routine, though, I need to have certain items on my nightstand before I go to sleep.

Throughout the day, I carry my binder and spiral notebook around with me. That notebook is my journal, but I also frequently use it to write the first drafts of blog posts, short stories and other pieces. If I always have it next to me, I can achieve #10.

10. Grab time.

I may be partial, but I think moms are the best at this. Every mom I know juggles dozens of responsibilities every day. We recognize time gifts wherever we are — during club meetings, practices, etc.; while our kids are taking tests or finishing independent work or waiting in pick-up lines. If you're a mom, know that I think you're a Wonder Woman! If you have a mom or know a mom, give her a hug today ... or coffee; moms run on coffee.

When my kids have activities, like book club, I take a packed bag with my laptop or trusty notebook for writing, revising or world-building. My notebook stays next to me while we do school. It gets tossed in my church bag, especially on the mornings I don't have to teach Sunday school. (I have been known to slip away and read or write during that time.)

It's easy for me to get frustrated when I only have five, ten or twenty minutes here and there. That doesn't feel like enough time to accomplish anything; however, if I'm organized, know my ultimate goals, plan ahead, choose the right activities and always stand ready to grab those time snip-its, I can maximize time in huge ways. And, so can you!

Appendix H: Joy's Case For Goals

Goal Requirements

SUCCESSFUL PEOPLE HAVE A REASON for their achievements—goal-setting and goal-keeping. We can chat all day about how much we want to accomplish this or that; but, until we set concrete and achievable goals, those remain simply happy daydreams. Strong, calculated goals force us to declare our intentions, affix a deadline to them and identify each step needed to achieve them.

You can't make a list of goals and expect them to magically happen, though. Goals require planning, preparation and perseverance.

PLANNING

I could set a goal like "Write a book." Sounds great, right? Wrong! It's too vague. One of our goals was to write this book and start an Author Resource Series. Beneath that giant goal came many mini-goals.

Mea and I first scheduled a brainstorming session. We made a list of topics for the series. After that, we researched our topics and picked one. Next, we compared our calendars and chose a date to virtually outline the book and then another date to meet up in person to write the first draft. Those are just the first few mini-goals that led to achieving the monster goals of writing this book to start a series.

I need to point out that goals must be fluid, even with their need for planning. They're rarely something you chisel into stone on December 31 and expect to roll into your "Done" garden the following December 31. While main goals may remain the same, mini-goals should always be written in pencil.

With this particular goal, we identified multiple steps toward achieving it, many of which we had to learn as we went, which meant our timelines were hazy. For such an uncertain path, I advise you to mentally prepare to adjust whatever you need to in order to reach this goal, regardless of how many erasers you go through.

Preparation

The preparation involved with achieving set goals varies. I mentioned research during the planning stage.

We had to research comparable book titles to our proposals. We chose the least-represented topic to tackle first, scratched off a few that seem oversaturated and put a few to the side to revisit once we're either more experienced or have a new take on the matter.

A list of mini-goals and careful research should be closely followed by setting personal deadlines and putting a plan together on a calendar.

However, a list of mini-goals remains as useless as discarded resolutions once the New Year's black-eyed peas' luck has worn off, when not accompanied by set completion dates and a plan of attack.

PERSEVERANCE

I would be happiest if I could set a schedule and stick to that same one for the next fifty years. The realization that plans and goals must be flexible causes a heart-sinking sensation that sends me grabbing for a stronghold.

If you're like me, breathe. Take a few moments. Grab a paper bag, if necessary. I'll be right here.

Understanding and admitting the necessity of being willing to adjust and adapt will set you free.

Do I do this perfectly? Am I cool as a cucumber when something derails all my pretty plans and messes up my delightfully colorful schedule? Nope. Not even close.

However, I've learned to breathe. Face the alteration with acceptance and take a few breaths before I get to work adjusting my expectations and plans. I have to be honest with you. Most of the time these unexpected turns in the maze end up making things go so much better with infinitely better timing than I could have ever planned—once I relax and accept them.

Most important, though, is to persevere. One of my largest goals over the next few years is to continue world-building and researching for an epic fantasy series. This is a goal I can't break down with much specificity yet.

I've never built complete worlds and creatures and histories and mythologies and languages before, so I have no clue how long that process will take me. My preparation begins with learning the process, reading the masters and giving it a shot here and there. I've been learning by writing short stories nearly every month.

I set aside specific times each month to create these pieces that I will stack together once I begin more focused writing. I can plan and schedule sessions to write these stories, explore my world or learn from others. One super-wee-mini-goal at a time for this giant dragon!

The next group in this goal's steps includes outlining and detailed plotting. At that point, I will plan dates to prepare further research and then begin writing as I persevere through each step to the end purpose. I'm realistic enough to realize a work like this won't fit neatly into a one-year timeline. J.R.R. Tolkien committed his entire writing life to *The Silmarillion* ... and never saw it in published form. I'll need a heap of perseverance to make this work happen.

While planning, preparation and perseverance are vital to pursuing our goals, we also need to understand three specifics about goals.

Goal Specifics

GOALS SHOULD BE ATTAINABLE.

In 2010, my family moved to the Greater New Orleans area. That was the first time I decided to let go of my excuses and pursue my dream of authorship. I sat down and jotted out my goals—one-year, five-year, ten-year, fifteen-year, twenty-year and even twenty-five-year goals. Writing out those goals was helpful and even smart in some ways. You see, it allowed me to see my desires and to isolate my passions. I looked into my future and pictured what I longed to see and then poured it out in ink.

Here's where I made my goal-setting mistake: I did not set *attainable* goals. I set big-picture, pie-in-the-sky goals without all the little stepping stone goals to get me there. For 2011 three goals I wrote were "write, complete three children's books," "submit one book" and "begin and keep up a collection of columns/blogs—at least fifty." Since I wrote these at the very beginning of 2011, these goals were actually realistic, and I did work toward them. However, I didn't sit down and calculate how many posts I would need to produce per week to hit my goal. With fifty-two weeks in a year, I should have assigned myself one post a week to write and one post a week to edit. Next, I should have made a list of topics to choose from. Upfront preparation would save time during my weekly blog-writing sessions. With that plan and preparation in place, I've switched an overwhelming goal to a simple weekly task I can attain.

GOALS REQUIRE A DEADLINE.

I cannot urge the importance of deadlines strongly enough. It could be the journalist in me, but deadlines drive me more than anything else. For my children's book goals, the goals themselves were not too bad. However, I was missing a deadline. I should have taken that goal and planned out my time. I could have set dates for first draft completions, dates for revisions, etc. For the one I chose to submit, I should have also set mini-goals of researching publishers (or agents) as well as dates for focus groups, further revisions and mailing out my hopes and dreams. (I originally planned to follow a traditional path to publication. I'll save my story to Indie publication for another book.)

GOALS NEED ENCOURAGEMENT.

As important as attainable goal-setting with set—yet flexible—deadlines is, a support system for you and your goals is equally important.

Who is your writing community? You could find them in your own family and friends first, then in writer acquaintances. Beyond them, the global world we live in teems with supportive groups willing to come alongside and encourage you. We mention several in Appendix I.

Wherever you find your support system, cherish and nurture those relationships and thank them by achieving your goals.

Appendix l: QWERTY-Recommended Resources

Craft Resources

The Story Grid: What Good Editors Know
Shawn Coyne

Story Genius: How to Use Brain Science to Go Beyond Outlining and Write a Riveting Novel
Lisa Cron

Wired for Story: The Writer's Guide to Using Brain Science to Hook Readers from the Very First Sentence
Lisa Cron

Save the Cat! The Last Book on Screenwriting You'll Ever Need
Blake Snyder

Save the Cat! Writes a Novel: The Last Book on Novel Writing You'll Ever Need
Jessica Brody

Bird by Bird: Some Instructions on Writing and Life
Anne Lamott

The Career Novelist: A Literary Agent Offers Strategies for Success
Donald Maass

Something Startling Happens: The 120 Story Beats Every Writer Needs to Know
Todd Klick

Fast-Draft Your Memoir: Write Your Life Story in 45 Hours
Rachael Herron

Creativity Resources

The Artist's Way: A Spiritual Path to Higher Creativity
Julia Cameron

The War of Art: Break Through the Blocks and Win Your Inner Creative Battles
Steven Pressfield

The Healthy Writer: Reduce Your Pain, Improve Your Health, and Build a Writing Career for the Long-Term
Joanna Penn & Dr. Euan Lawson

Critique-Type Resources

How to Write Non-Fiction: Turn Your Knowledge Into Words
Joanna Penn

The Curiosities: A Collection of Stories
Maggie Stiefvater, Tessa Gratton, Brenna Yovanoff

The Anatomy of Curiosity
Maggie Stiefvater, Tessa Gratton, Brenna Yovanoff

Self-Editing and Revision Resources

Your Favorite dictionary and thesaurus

The Chicago Manual of Style
The University of Chicago Press

Revision & Self-Editing: Techniques for Transforming Your First Draft into a Finished Novel
James Scott Bell

On Writing Well: The Classic Guide to Writing Nonfiction
William Zinsser

The Elements of Style
William Strunk and E.B. White

Online Writing Courses

Holly Lisle's Writing Courses
https://hollyswritingclasses.com/

The Creative Penn Courses by Joanna Penn
https://thecreativepenn.com/courses

Wired for Story: How to Become a Story Genius
https://www.creativelive.com/business/writing-classes/wired-for-story-lisa-cron

Write Your Book: Start Strong and Get It Done
https://www.creativelive.com/class/write-your-book-start-strong-and-get-going-jennie-nash

Write Publish Sell Courses
https://writepublishsell.thinkific.com/collections

Publication Method Resources

Publishing 101: A First-Time Author's Guide to Getting Published, Marketing and Promoting Your Book, and Building a Successful Career
Jane Friedman

The Business of Being a Writer
Jane Friedman

Business for Authors: How to Be an Author Entrepreneur
Joanna Penn

Successful Self-Publishing: How to Self-Publish and Market Your Book
Joanna Penn

QWERTY-Approved Online Writing Groups

Writer Moms Inc.
https://www.writermomsinc.com
Active on Facebook, Twitter and Instagram

Motivated Writer
https://www.facebook.com/groups/motivatedwriter/
Active on Facebook with weekly check-ins for goals and achievements

Women In Publishing
https://www.facebook.com/WomenInPublishing/
Excellent opportunities to network; purchase of the All Access Pass to the annual online Women In Publishing Summit grants access to a members-only group with even more chances to connect

Writer Mom Life
http://writermomlife.com
Active primarily on Facebook; Podcast geared toward Indie Author Moms

The Writing Pack
https://www.victoriagriffin.net/pack.html
Active on Facebook and website

QWERTY-Vetted Critique Partner Matching Sites

https://www.writeoncon.org/cpmatch/

> WriteOnCon is a well-known, online writing conference. In 2018 they introduced their critique partner matchup, which helps pair authors who write picture books, early readers, chapter books, middle grade and young adult.

https://www.critiquecircle.com/

> This website skips right to the critique trial. You can upload a piece needing critique and see what type of response you get. You may find someone who comments on your story that would like to become permanent critique partners, which is the goal of *Finders Keepers*. Your story is public to the critique circle community, so be prepared to receive and process multiple perspectives.

http://www.kidlit411.com/p/ms-swap.html Kidlit411

> Kidlit411.com is a website that compiles helpful information regarding writing and publishing to save authors time in research. This is a platform already, but then they go a step further. The manuscript swap Facebook page hosted by Kidlit411 is a helpful resource to get initial critiques and, hopefully, introduce like-minded authors to each other, beginning a critique partnership.

https://groups.google.com/forum/?utm_source=digest&utm_medium=email#!forum/critique-partner-matchup/topics

> This Google forum was created by author Maggie Stiefvater, an advocate of critique partnerships. Post information about your manuscript and browse other synopses to find one that strikes your fancy. There's a good

chance your future critique partner is behind one of those descriptions.

https://www.facebook.com/groups/betareaderconnect/

BetaReader Connect helps you link up with beta readers and critique partners through Facebook. There's a structure to what you post regarding your manuscript and the requirements fall nicely with what we recommend in *Finders Keepers*—genre, synopsis, word count, time frame and the like. The administrators are also part of https://betareader.io/ which is a website that monitors how much your betas and critique partners read on what days and provides a platform for in-text comments and broad view questions. It's a little micro-managey but could be perfect for more detail-oriented writers.

Appendix J: Critique Partner Contract

THE FOLLOWING CONTRACT MAY be used by critique partners who would like to add a level of formality to their relationship and an extra layer of clarity on their purpose and commitment to one another.

This may also serve as a good reminder for all critique partners to review once in a while. It will be an outline for how they should approach their commitments and how they can practice the example of critique partnerships presented in *Finders Keepers*.

By committing to this relationship with such seriousness, each writer showcases a deep desire to uphold the promises made.

Appendix J: Critique Partner Contract

I, _____, do hereby enter into this *Critique Partner Relationship* with _____ to improve the writers and our writing to the benefit of each of us in our creative processes and for all future readers.

I further commit to be a *Critique Partner* who, as a knowledgeable writer, desires to assist other writers with their works and willingly accept reciprocation, creating a harmonious relationship that results in literature superior to what we, the authors alone, could provide for our readers.

I promise to embrace my critique partner as a friend and treat him/her with compassion, forgiveness and grace while giving him/her respectful truth from a place of love. I will practice gracious acceptance of a critique and patience for the delivery of one.

I promise to set hubris aside. I will be open and honest about both my strengths and weaknesses. I will reward the time my partner puts into critiquing my piece by weighing his/her suggestions without stacking the other side of the scale with my own weights of laziness, pride or stubbornness.

I commit myself to my partner and his/her work. I will care as deeply about his/her project as I care for my own. I will be there to push and drive, supporting his/her efforts to be the best author he/she can. I will cheer him/her on as his/her words find their ways into the hearts of readers.

I promise to maintain honesty and openness in this partnership through clear and careful communication as I willingly continue to learn and grow in my craft knowledge and industry understanding for the benefit of my writing, our partnership and future readers.

Should life circumstances alter our plans and my commitment, I will be upfront and honest concerning those changes as soon as possible, fulfill any promises made to the best of my ability and strive to continue support in some manner, if possible. If such changes should affect my partner, I will be understanding and empathetic with the situation.

Signed: _____

Dated: _____

Glossary of QWERTY Definitions

The **ANTAGONIST** is the person or thing that hinders your protagonist from getting what he wants, as he simultaneously pursues his own desire.

AUTHOR VOICE contains the natural sentence structure and word choices unique to an author when he writes. These preferences typically follow the writer across his works.

A **CHARACTER ARC** is the internal, emotional change of a character from the beginning of a story to its end as a response to trials and circumstances in the character's path.

CHARACTER DEVELOPMENT is the work an author does to portray a character, whether fictional or real, as true to life through details such as the emotional change from beginning to end, subtleties in personality and internal complexities.

CONFLICT is created by the obstacles that prevent the characters from getting what they desire.

A **CONNECTING THREAD** is the central idea or question that connects the work from beginning to end.

A **CRITIQUE PARTNER** (CP) should be a knowledgeable writer who desires to assist other writers with their works and willingly accepts reciprocation, creating a harmonious relationship that results in literature superior to what the author alone could provide for readers.

The **CRITIQUE PARTNER RELATIONSHIP** exists to improve the writer and the writing to the benefit of each person involved in the creative process and for all future readers.

GENRE is the label addressing the content of a piece, so people who like to read in a particular field will find it, bookstores will know how to shelve it and digital retailers will know how to list it. For the writer, genre informs him of reader expectations a piece should fulfill. It can guide plot, character motivation and resolution.

MOOD is the emotion or emotions evoked in the reader by the story's prose. This aspect is subjective; however, some universal conclusions may be drawn regarding the mood of a piece.

The **MOTIVATION** behind a piece is the author's driving reason for writing it in the first place. This might be where the author's worldview most comes into play.

NARRATIVE TONE is revealed in the consistent emotions the author evokes, generally when he writes in third person omniscient or third person close. These points of view especially highlight the author's voice. Narrative tone is a concoction of the author's word choice, syntax and story.

NARRATIVE VOICE is the worldview, cadence and word choice the author uses for the story's narrator.

PLOT is the ordering of events or happenings in a story that leads to the ultimate resolution and hosts the character arc journey.

PLOT POINTS are main events or happenings that are necessary to character development and plot and act as story guides. Example plot points are exposition (introduction), inciting incident (where the main character is moved to action), climax (intense moment where trouble is faced) and denouement (resolution).

PLOT THREADS link a character to each conflict from the beginning of the piece to the end of it through each plot point. A character can have multiple plot threads.

The **PROTAGONIST** is the main character of the story who has a desperate desire for something seemingly out of reach. This should be the character with the most internal change in the story.

The **PURPOSE** of a piece is what the author wants his audience to take away from his writing.

A **SERIES** is a story told over multiple books or articles that depend on each other for a complete understanding.

A **STANDALONE** is a book in which the story's understanding and resolution is not dependent on another book.

STORY is a series of struggles and complications concerning real or fictional characters, organized and expressed in a way to elicit a mindset shift or emotional response for a variety of reasons—escapism, curiosity, distraction, morality or persuasion, for example.

STORY STRUCTURE is the way in which an author chooses to present his tale.

SUBTEXT is dialogue that both means what it means and means something deeper.

THEME encompasses the central topic on which a manuscript focuses. It's the glue that holds all the pieces and parts of the writing together, giving the project purpose. Theme affects the author's words and mood choices, character development, plot development—pretty much all aspects of the story. Depending on the author's purpose and genre, theme can be exemplified through character experiences or presented in a thesis statement. Theme may be an exploration of a broad idea like *sacrifice* or of something specific, like *repressing emotions doesn't heal them*.

CRITIQUE TYPES

An **AUTHOR VOICE AND NARRATIVE TONE CRITIQUE** analyzes each technique respectively and determines consistency in each.

A **CHARACTER DEVELOPMENT ANALYSIS AND CRITIQUE** examines the consistency of a character's speech, interactions, actions and reactions as well as the strength of his internal change over the course of his story. This critique can focus on the protagonist, antagonist or all named or vital characters.

A **DIALOGUE REVIEW CRITIQUE** focuses on consistency in the characters' voices, with particular attention given to the dialogue's purpose, place and conciseness, as well as its natural presentation and flow.

A **NONFICTION CRITIQUE** often requires a more overall approach and necessitates that the evaluator considers the piece's purpose, topic relevance, structure and logical progress, primary question (and its resulting answer or answers) and clarity in the author's point of view.

An **OVERALL CONTENT EVALUATION CRITIQUE** is what we like to call "the whole shebang." This critique reviews the entire project—theme clarity, story structure, dialogue, character depth and development, plot development and logical consistency, author voice and narrative tone, point of view and pacing, to name a few.

A **PACING REVIEW CRITIQUE** measures the speed of every scene and determines if it's too fast, too slow or perfect to fit that scene's needs.

A **PLOT DEVELOPMENT CRITIQUE** weighs the worth of each event—large or small, mostly external but potentially internal, too—against its ability to move the story forward. This critique also uncovers inconsistencies or "holes" in the story.

A **POINT OF VIEW (POV) CONSISTENCY CRITIQUE** checks that the story is told from the same perspective throughout or is consistently and smoothly divided among various points of view.

A **THEME INTEGRATION CRITIQUE** dissects how the theme is represented in each chapter or scene and across the entire work.

Sources

Campbell, Joseph. *The Hero with a Thousand Faces*. Novato, CA: New World Library, 2008.

Coyne, Shawn. *The Story Grid: What Good Editors Know*. New York: Black Irish Entertainment, 2015.

Kubrick, Stanley. *The Shining*. DVD. Directed by Stanley Kubrick. 1980.

Maslow, A. H. "A theory of human motivation." *Psychological Review, 50 (1943):* 370-96.

Penn, Joanna. *How to Write Non-Fiction: Turn Your Knowledge Into Words*. Curl Up Press, 2018.

Rancatore, Joy E. *Any Good Thing*. Slidell, LA: Logos & Mythos Press, 2019.

Rancatore, Joy E. *Plus One Year More*. Slidell, LA: Logos & Mythos Press, 2019.

Ritchey, Rachael. *The Crux Anthology*. Newman Lake, WA: RR Publishing, 2018.

Stallone, Sylvester. *Rocky III*. DVD. Directed by Sylvester Stallone. 1982.

Szabo, Thomas and Hélène Giraud. *Minuscule: Valley of the Lost Ants*. DVD. Directed by Hélène Giraud and Thomas Szabo. 2014.

Whedon, Joss, et al. *Firefly*. DVDs. Directed by Joss Whedon, et al. 2002-2003.

Zaleski, Philip and Carol Zaleski. *The Fellowship: The Literary Lives of the Inklings: J.R.R. Tolkien, C. S. Lewis, Owen Barfield, Charles Williams*. New York: Farrar, Straus and Giroux, 2015.

About the Author

JOY E. RANCATORE is an Indie Author and the owner of Logos & Mythos Press in the Greater New Orleans area. She entered the professional writing world at age sixteen with a small-town weekly newspaper where the editor consistently ran her byline as Joe E. Over the years, Joy has written for newspapers, magazines and blogs, worked in public relations, web design and customer support and freelanced as a writer, editor and photographer. She writes fiction, nonfiction and everything between. She is the author of *Any Good Thing*, 2019, and *Plus One Year More*, 2020, and a contributing author to *The Crux Anthology*, 2018. In addition to her publishing roles, Joy is a blogger, speaker, teacher, editor for fellow Indie Authors and co-host of QWERTY Writing Life Podcast.

When Joy's not doing horrible things to her characters or dreaming up faerie creatures and fantastic weapons, she hangs out with her husband Tony, homeschools her two children, snuggles her two stinky dogs and lets her cat, Tolkien, do whatever he wants. They'd prefer to live in Middle-earth or Narnia or Hogwarts or in a galaxy far, far away; but, for now, they're living their happily ever after in the Camellia City across Lake Pontchartrain from New Orleans.

Visit Joy:

www.joyerancatore.com
www.facebook.com/joyerancatore
www.twitter.com/joyerancatore
www.instagram.com/joyerancatore
www.goodreads.com/joyerancatore
www.pinterest.com/joyerancatore
www.linkedin.com/in/joyerancatore

About the Author

MEAGAN (MEA) SMITH lives in a wooden house on a hill and trips over a multitude of cats while parenting her two rambunctious boys. When her mind floats too far from home, her caring husband tugs on her soul-string and, then, grills her chicken for dinner.

Finding joy in a multitude of creative practices, Mea is a published author who co-hosts QWERTY Writing Life podcast with her critique partner, Joy E. Rancatore. Other creative avenues Mea enjoys are visual art, songwriting, photography, jewelry making, and quilting. She speaks to audiences on the topics of creative writing, embracing creativity, nurturing critique partnerships, and writing through grief. Mea earned a Master's in English, though considers herself a perpetual student.

Over the years, Mea's nonfiction works have focused on the writing craft and life lessons, delivered with kindness, humor, and honesty. She believes love doesn't deter hateful things from happening, but it always conquers them. Because of this, she continues to create fictional content tinted with hope, preferring her tales set in contemporary and/or fantastical places. Her poetry is based on a true story. Always.

If you're in south Mississippi, you can find Mea watching fireflies from her back porch or wandering the aisles of her local library.

Visit Mea:
www.measmith.com
www.facebook.com/meathewriter
www.twitter.com/mea_smith
www.instagram.com/measmithwrites

QWERTY Speaking Availability

In Person or Online

Potential Topics:
- Critique Partnerships
- Co-Authoring
- Candid Chats about Creativity
- Writing Workshops

Email for availability:
editorial@logosandmythospress.com

QWERTY Writing Life Podcast

New Episodes
Every Tuesday

Find Links to All Major Podcast Portals and YouTube:
www.logosandmythospress.com/qwerty-writing-life

Logos & Mythos Press

Editing Services
for *INDIE AUTHORS*

Packages & Payment Plans
FREE Evaluation

Editing with Quality for You

www.logosandmythospress.com/editing
editorial@logosandmythospress.com

Notes

Notes

Notes

Finders Keepers: A Practical Approach To Find And Keep Your Writing Critique Partner

Notes

LOGOS & MYTHOS PRESS

SLIDELL, LA, USA

www.ingramcontent.com/pod-product-compliance
Lightning Source LLC
Chambersburg PA
CBHW052009070526
44584CB00016B/1676